History and Culture of Honduras

The People, Independence, The Society, Ethnic Groups, and Politics.

Written
by
Caleb Roberts

Publisher
Word Print.
73 Main Road, Auchenbrack, DG3 1HW
United Kingdom

..

Table of Content

Honduras

The History

Honduras has been an undeveloped country for much of its history. Its steep geography, along with a scarcity of excellent ports on the Pacific coast, has kept it largely isolated from the mainstream of social and economic growth. Tegucigalpa, the capital, is positioned high in the middle highlands, away from the major north-south transit arteries of the isthmus.

Honduras' harsh geography and semi-isolation have offered both benefits and problems. Honduras, unlike its neighboring republics of El Salvador and Guatemala, did not establish a completely dominating landholding oligarchy. It also avoided the squabbles over transisthmian transit routes that afflicted Nicaragua and Panama. Finally, unlike the other Central American countries, Honduras is not dominated by a single city. Because of the capital's seclusion, San Pedro Sula rose to prominence as the nation's commercial and industrial hub in the twentieth century.

However, lack of growth resulted in relatively weak social and political institutions during most of Honduras' history. Long periods of political insecurity, multiple military coups, and significant government corruption and incompetence have characterized most of the country's history. External forces have repeatedly exploited and exacerbated these issues. Neighboring Central American countries have regularly engaged in Honduran

1

domestic affairs, instilling fear among Hondurans of foreign aggression. Countries outside the area have also exploited Honduran politics to suit their own national interests on occasion. During the first part of the twentieth century, the United Fruit Corporate and the Standard Fruit Company controlled the Honduran economy to such an extent that company executives were commonly viewed as wielding as much influence as the Honduran president. Increased nationalism and economic diversification have modified the situation in subsequent decades, but Honduras remained a country very vulnerable to and reliant on foreign factors in the early 1990s. Honduras remains impoverished and vulnerable despite national and international efforts. In the 1980s, security concerns were focused on the Nicaraguan border; in the early 1990s, concerns were focused on El Salvador due to insurgency issues and a border dispute with Honduras.

Honduras, both a product and a victim of its past, was attempting in the mid-1990s to find a way to reap the benefits of modernization while avoiding the violent conflicts that afflicted its neighbors in the 1980s.

Pre-Columbian Society

The Mayan Heritage

Pre-Columbian Honduras was populated by a complex mixture of indigenous peoples representing a wide variety of cultural backgrounds and linguistic groups the most advanced and notable of which were related to the Maya of the Yucatán and Guatemala. Mayan civilization had reached western Honduras in the fifth century A.D., probably spreading from lowland Mayan centers in Guatemala's Petén region. The Maya spread rapidly through the Río Motagua Valley, centering their control on the major ceremonial center of Copán, near the present-day town of Santa Rosa de Copán. For three and a half centuries, the Maya developed the city, making it one of the principal centers of their culture. At one point, Copán was probably the leading center for both astronomical studies in which the Maya were quite advanced and art. One of the longest Mayan hieroglyphic inscriptions ever discovered was found at Copán. The Maya also established extensive trade networks spanning as far as central Mexico.

Then, at the height of the Mayan civilization, Copán was apparently abandoned. The last dated hieroglyph in Copán is 800 A.D. Much of the population evidently remained in the area after that, but the educated class the priests and rulers who built the temples, inscribed the glyphs, and developed the astronomy and mathematics suddenly vanished. Copán fell into ruin, and the descendants of the Maya who remained had no memory of the meanings of the inscriptions or of the reasons for the sudden fall.

Other Indigenous Groups

Following the period of Mayan dominance, the area that would eventually comprise Honduras was occupied by a multiplicity of indigenous peoples. Indigenous groups related to the Toltec of central Mexico migrated from the northwest into parts of what became western and southern Honduras. Most notable were the Toltecspeaking Chorotega, who established themselves near the present-day city of Choluteca. Later enclaves of Nahua-speaking peoples, such as the Pipil, whose language was related to that of the Aztec, established themselves at various locations from the Caribbean coast to the Golfo de Fonseca on the Pacific coast.

While groups related to indigenous peoples of Mexico moved into western and southern Honduras, other peoples with languages related to those of the Chibcha of Colombia were establishing themselves in areas that became northeastern Honduras. Most prominent among these were the Ulva and Paya speakers. Along the Caribbean coast, a variety of groups settled. Most important were the Sumu, who were also located in Nicaragua, and the Jicaque, whose language family has been a source of debate among scholars. Finally, in parts of what is now west-central Honduras were the Lenca, who also were believed to have migrated north from Colombia but whose language shows little relation to any other indigenous group.

Although divided into numerous distinct and frequently hostile groups, the indigenous inhabitants of preconquest Honduras (before the early 1500s) carried on considerable trade with other parts of their immediate region as well as with areas as far away as Panama and Mexico. Although it appears that no major cities were in existence at the time of the conquest, the total population was nevertheless fairly high. Estimates range up to 2 million, although the actual figure was probably nearer to 500,000.

Spanish Conquest and Settlement

The Initial Explorations

European contacts with the indigenous population of Honduras began with the final voyage of Christopher Columbus. In 1502 Columbus sailed past the Islas de la Bahía (Bay Islands) and shortly thereafter reached the mainland of Central America. While at one of the islands, Columbus discovered and seized a large canoe loaded with a wide variety of trade goods. Evidence seems to indicate that the canoe's occupants were Mayan traders and that their encounter with Columbus marked his first direct contact with the civilizations of Mexican and northern Central America. Despite the fact that the canoe had been observed coming from the west, Columbus turned east and then south, sailing away from the civilizations and doing little exploring on the Honduran coast. His only direct legacy was the assigning of a few place names on the Caribbean coast, notably Guanaja for one of the Islas de la Bahía, Cabo Gracias a Dios for the eastern extremity of Honduras, and Honduras (depths in Spanish) for the overall region. The latter name suggests the deep waters off the northern coast.

Little exploration took place for the next two decades. Spanish navigators Juan Díaz de Solís and Vicente Yáñez Pinzón probably touched on part of the Honduran coast in 1508 but devoted most of their efforts to exploring farther north. Some expeditions from the islands of Cuba and Hispaniola may have reached the mainland and certainly began to decimate the population of the Islas de la Bahía in the second decade of the century, but otherwise the Honduran Caribbean coast was a neglected area.

Interest in the mainland was dramatically revived as a result of the expedition of Hernán Cortés to Mexico. While Cortés was completing his conquest of the Aztec, expeditions from Mexico, Panama, and the Caribbean began to move into Central America. In 1523 part of an expedition headed by Gil González Dávila discovered the Golfo de Fonseca on the Pacific coast, naming it in honor of Bishop Rodríguez de Fonseca. The following year, four separate Spanish land expeditions began the conquest of Honduras.

The Era of the Conquistadores

The nearly simultaneous invasions of Honduras in 1524 by rival Spanish expeditions began an era of conflict among rival Spanish claimants as well as with the indigenous population. The major initial expeditions were led by González Dávila, who hoped to carve out a territory for his own rule, and by Cristóbal de Olid, who was dispatched from Cuba by Cortés. Once in Honduras, however, Olid succumbed to personal ambition and attempted to establish his own independent authority. Word of this reached Cortés in Mexico, and to restore his own authority, he ordered yet another expedition, this one under the command of Francisco de Las Casas. Then, doubting the trustworthiness of any subordinate, Cortés set out for Honduras himself. The situation was further complicated by the entry into Honduras of expeditions from Guatemala under Pedro de Alvarado and from Nicaragua under Hernando de Soto.

In the initial struggle for power, Olid seemed to gain the upper hand, capturing both González Dávila and Las Casas. His captives, however, having managed to subvert the loyalty of some of Olid's men, took Olid prisoner, and then promptly beheaded him. Although later condemned for this action by a Mexican court, none of the conspirators ever suffered any real punishment.

The arrival of Cortés in Honduras in 1525 temporarily restored some order to the Spanish conquest. He established his own authority over the rival claimants, obtained the submission of numerous indigenous chiefs, and tried to promote the creation of Spanish towns. His own headquarters was located at Trujillo on the Caribbean coast. In April 1526, Cortés returned to Mexico, and the remaining Spaniards resumed their strife.

Some order was again restored in October of that year when the first royal governor, Diego López de Salcedo, arrived. López de Salcedo's policies, however, drove many indigenous people, once pacified by Cortés, into open revolt. His attempt to extend his jurisdiction into Nicaragua resulted in his imprisonment by the authorities there. After agreeing to a Nicaraguan-imposed definition of the boundary between the two provinces, López de Salcedo was released but did not return to Honduras until 1529.

The early 1530s were not prosperous for Honduras. Renewed fighting among the Spaniards, revolts, and decimation of the settled indigenous population through disease, mistreatment, and exportation of large numbers to the Caribbean islands as slaves left the colony on the edge of collapse by 1534. The Spanish crown renamed the depressed province as Honduras-Higueras, subdividing it into two districts. Higueras encompassed the western part while the rest remained known as Honduras. The decline in population of the province continued, and only the direct intervention of Pedro de Alvarado from Guatemala in 1536 kept Higueras from being abandoned. Alvarado was attracted by the prospect of gold in the region, and, with the help of native Guatemalans who accompanied him, he soon developed a profitable gold-mining industry centered in the newly established town of Gracias.

The discovery of gold and silver deposits attracted new settlers and increased the demand for indigenous labor. The enforced labor, however, led to renewed resistance by the native people that culminated in a major uprising in 1537. The leader of the uprising was a capable young Lenca chieftain known as Lempira (after whom the Honduran national monetary unit would eventually be named). Lempira established his base on a fortified hill known as the Peñol de Cerquín and until 1538 successfully defeated all efforts to subdue him. Inspired by his examples, other native inhabitants began revolting, and the entire district of Higueras seemed imperiled. Lempira was ultimately murdered while negotiating with the Spaniards. After his death, resistance rapidly disintegrated, although some fighting continued through 1539.

The defeat of Lempira's revolt accelerated the decimation of the indigenous population. In 1539 an estimated 15,000 native Americans remained under Spanish control; two years later, there were only 8,000. Most of these were divided into *encomiendas*, a system that left the native people in their villages but placed them under the control of individual Spanish settlers. Under terms of the *encomienda* system, the Spaniards were supposed to provide the indigenous people with religious instruction and collect tribute from them for the crown. In return, the Spaniards were entitled to a supposedly limited use of indigenous labor. As the native population declined, the settlers exploited those remaining even more ruthlessly. This exploitation led to a clash between the Spanish settlers and authorities on one side and on the other side the Roman Catholic Church led by Father Cristóbal de Pedraza, who, in 1542 became the first bishop of Honduras. Bishop Pedraza, like others after him, had little success in his efforts to protect the native people.

Colonial Honduras

The Spread of Colonization and the Growth of Mining

The defeat of Lempira's revolt, the establishment of the bishopric (first at Trujillo, then at Comayagua after Pedraza's death), and the decline in fighting among rival Spanish factions all contributed to expanded settlement and increased economic activity in the 1540s. A variety of agricultural activities was developed, including cattle ranching and, for a time, the harvesting of large quantities of sasparilla root. But the key economic activity of sixteenth-century Honduras was mining gold and silver.

The initial mining centers were located near the Guatemalan border, around Gracias. In 1538 these mines produced significant quantities of gold. In the early 1540s, the center for mining shifted eastward to the Río Guayape Valley, and silver joined gold as a major product. This change contributed to the rapid decline of Gracias and the rise of Comayagua as the center of colonial Honduras. The demand for labor also led to further revolts and accelerated the decimation of the native population. As a result, African slavery was introduced into Honduras, and by 1545 the province may have had as many as 2,000 slaves. Other gold deposits were found near San Pedro Sula and the port of Trujillo.

By the late 1540s, Honduras seemed headed for relative prosperity and influence, a development marked by the establishment in 1544 of the regional *audiencia* of Guatemala with its capital at Gracias, Honduras. The *audiencia* was a Spanish governmental unit encompassing both judicial and legislative functions whose president held the additional titles of governor and captain general (hence the alternative name of Captaincy General of Guatemala). The location of the capital was bitterly resented by the more populous centers in Guatemala and El Salvador, and in 1549 the capital of the *audiencia* was moved to Antigua, Guatemala.

Mining production began to decline in the 1560s, and Honduras rapidly declined in importance. The subordination of Honduras to the Captaincy General of Guatemala had been reaffirmed with the move of the capital to Antigua, and the status of Honduras as a province within the Captaincy General of Guatemala would be maintained until independence. Beginning in 1569, new silver strikes in the interior briefly revived the economy and led to the founding of the town of Tegucigalpa, which soon began to rival Comayagua as the most important town in the province. But the silver boom peaked in 1584, and economic depression returned shortly thereafter. Mining efforts in Honduras were hampered by a lack of capital and labor, difficult terrain, the limited size of many gold and silver deposits, and bureaucratic regulations and incompetence. Mercury, vital to the production of silver, was constantly in short supply; once an entire year's supply was lost through the negligence of officials. By the seventeenth century, Honduras had become a poor and neglected backwater of the Spanish colonial empire, having a scattered population of mestizos, native people, blacks, and a handful of Spanish rulers and landowners.

Colonial Society, Economy, and Government

Although mining provided much of the limited revenue Honduras generated for the Spanish crown, a majority of the inhabitants were engaged in agriculture. Attempts to promote agricultural exports had limited success, however, and most production remained on a subsistence level. If anything, the province became more rural during the seventeenth and eighteenth centuries. As a result of economic declines or foreign attacks, several town governments simply ceased to function during this period.

The cattle industry was probably the most important agricultural activity. Much of the cattle industry was on a small scale, but by 1714 six ranchers in the areas of the present-day departments of Yoro and Olancho owned over 1,000 head of cattle each. Some of the cattle were driven to Guatemala for sale. Such sales, however, occasionally produced meat shortages in Honduras and led to conflicts between Guatemalan and Honduran provincial officials.

Much of the Honduran interior remained uncolonized and outside of effective Spanish control during the colonial era. The Jicaque, fleeing into the hills, managed to retain considerable cultural autonomy. Other indigenous groups, however, were increasingly brought under Spanish influence and began to lose their separate identities. This assimilation was facilitated by occasional expeditions of government and church officials into new areas. One such expedition into Yoro in 1689 found forty villages of native people living outside of effective Spanish control.

By the end of the seventeenth century, governing Honduras had become a frustrating, thankless task. Only Comayagua, with 144 families, and Tegucigalpa, with 135, had over 100 Spanish settlers. The province boasted little in the way of education or culture. The lack of good ports, especially on the Pacific coast, limited contacts with the outside world. Whenever possible, the Spanish colonists forced native people to move to the Tegucigalpa area, where they were available for labor in the mines. However, illegal resettlement and corruption in the mining industry where every available ruse was used to avoid paying taxes created a constant series of problems for colonial authorities. Smuggling, especially on the Caribbean coast, was also a serious problem.

Early in the eighteenth century, the Bourbon Dynasty, linked to the rulers of France, replaced the Habsburgs on the throne of Spain and brought change to Honduras. The new dynasty began a series of reforms throughout the empire designed to make administration more efficient and profitable and to facilitate the defense of the colonies. Among these reforms was a reduction in the tax on precious minerals and in the cost of mercury, which was a royal monopoly. In Honduras these reforms contributed to a revival of the mining industry in the 1730s. Efforts to promote the Honduran tobacco industry as a royal monopoly proved less effective and encountered stiff local opposition. The same was true of plans to improve tax collection. Ultimately, the Bourbons abolished most of the corrupt local governmental units, replacing them in 1787 with a system of *intendencias* (the name of the new local unit and also its administrator, a royal official who supervised tax collections and commercial matters, controlled prices and credit, and exercised some judicial functions).

Anglo-Spanish Rivalry

A major problem for Spanish rulers of Honduras was the activity of the English along the northern Caribbean coast. These activities began in the late sixteenth century and continued into the nineteenth century. In the early years, Dutch as well as English corsairs (pirates) attacked the Caribbean coast, but as time passed the threat came almost exclusively from the English. In 1643 one English expedition destroyed the town of Trujillo, the major port for Honduras, leaving it virtually abandoned for over a century.

Destructive as they were, raiding expeditions were lesser problems than other threats. Beginning in the seventeenth century, English efforts to plant colonies along the Caribbean coast and in the Islas de la Bahía threatened to cut Honduras off from the Caribbean and raised the possibility of the loss of much of its territory. The English effort on the Honduran coast was heavily dependent on the support of groups known as the Sambo and the Miskito, racially mixed peoples of native American and African ancestry who were usually more than willing to attack Spanish settlements. British settlers were interested largely in trading, lumbering, and producing pitch. During the numerous eighteenth-century wars between Britain and Spain, however, the British crown found any activity that challenged Spanish hegemony on the Caribbean coast of Central America to be desirable.

Major British settlements were established at Cabo Gracias a Dios and to the west at the mouth of the Río Sico, as well as on the

Islas de la Bahía. By 1759 a Spanish agent estimated the population in the Río Sico area as 3,706.

Under the Bourbons, the revitalized Spanish government made several efforts to regain control over the Caribbean coast. In 1752 a major fort was constructed at San Fernando de Omoa near the Guatemalan border. In 1780 the Spanish returned in force to Trujillo, which they began developing as a base for expeditions against British settlements to the east. During the 1780s, the Spanish regained control over the Islas de la Bahía and drove the majority of the British and their allies out of the area around Black River. A British expedition briefly recaptured Black River, but the terms of the Anglo-Spanish Convention of 1786 gave definitive recognition to Spanish sovereignty over the Caribbean coast.

The Early Independence Years, 1821-99

The Collapse of Spanish Rule

In the early nineteenth century, Spanish power went into rapid decline. Although Spain was allied with France during the Napoleonic Wars, in 1808 Napoleon Bonaparte forced the Spanish king to abdicate and put a Bonaparte on the Spanish throne. In response, Spanish people erupted in revolt in Madrid and throughout Spain, setting off a chain of uprisings in Latin America. In Honduras, resentment against rule by the exiled Spanish king increased rapidly, especially because increased taxes for Spain's struggle against the French threatened the cattle industry. In 1812 disturbances that broke out in Tegucigalpa were more linked to long-standing rivalry with Comayagua, however, than to opposition to Spanish rule. The disturbances were quickly controlled, and, to appease local discontent, the municipal government of Tegucigalpa was reestablished.

The rivalry between Tegucigalpa and Comayagua helped precipitate the final collapse of Spanish authority in Honduras. A new Spanish administration attempted to transfer Comayagua's tobacco factory to Tegucigalpa. This move led to defiance by Comayagua, which refused to acknowledge the authority of the government in Guatemala. The weakened Spanish government was unable to end Comayagua's defiance, and for a time civil strife threatened to break out. Conflict was averted by the decision made by all the Central American provinces on September 15, 1821, to declare their independence from Spain. This action failed to resolve the dispute between Tegucigalpa and Comayagua, however; the former now urged the creation of a unified Central American state, while the latter favored union with the Empire of Mexico under the rule of General Augustín de Iturbide. Ultimately, Comayagua's position prevailed, and in early 1822 the Central American provinces declared their allegiance to Mexico.

This union lasted just over a year and produced few if any benefits for either party. In March 1823, Iturbide was overthrown in Mexico, and the empire was replaced by a republic. The Central American Congress, in which Comayagua but not Tegucigalpa was represented, was quickly convened. With little debate, the United Provinces of Central America declared their independence from Mexico. Mexico's only effort to reverse this decision consisted in maintaining control over Chiapas, the northernmost of the six previous provinces of Central America.

The United Provinces of Central America

From its 1823 inception, the new federation (the United Provinces of Central America) faced a series of ultimately unresolvable problems. Instead of engendering a spirit of unity, Spanish rule had fostered divisions and local suspicions. In the case of Honduras, this divisiveness was epitomized by the rivalry between Tegucigalpa and Comayagua. There was even some sentiment for admitting these two cities as separate provinces within the federation, but that proposal was ultimately rejected. In addition, much of the region was suspicious of Guatemalan ambitions to dominate Central America and wished to retain all possible local authority rather than surrender any to a central government.

At least equally serious was the division of the politically active population into conservative and liberal factions. The conservatives favored a more centralized government; a proclerical policy, including a church monopoly over education; and a more aristocratic form of government based on traditional Spanish values. The liberals wanted greater local autonomy and a restricted role for the church, as well as political and economic development as in the United States and parts of Western Europe. The conservatives favored keeping native people in their traditional, subservient position, while the liberals aimed at eventually eliminating indigenous society by incorporating it into the national, Hispanic culture.

At the time of Central American independence (1823), Honduras was among the least-developed and least-populated provinces. In 1824 its population was estimated at just over 137,000. Despite its meager population, Honduras produced two of the most prominent leaders of the federation, the liberal Francisco Morazán (nicknamed the "George Washington of Central America") and the conservative José Cecilio del Valle. In 1823 del Valle was narrowly defeated by liberal Manuel José Arce for election as the federation's first president. Morazán overthrew Arce in 1829 and was elected president of the federation in 1830, defeating del Valle.

The beginning of Morazán's administration in 1830 saw some efforts to reform and promote education. Success was limited, however, because of lack of funds and internal fighting. In the elections of 1834, del Valle defeated Morazán, but del Valle died before taking office, and the legislature offered Morazán the presidency. With clerical support, a conservative uprising began in Guatemala in 1837, and within a year the federation had begun to dissolve. On May 30, 1838, the Central American Congress removed Morazán from office, declared that the individual states could establish their own governments, and on July 7 recognized these as "sovereign, free, and independent political bodies."

The Development of an Independent Nation, 1838-99

For Honduras, the period of federation had been disastrous. Local rivalries and ideological disputes had produced political chaos and disrupted the economy. The British had taken advantage of the chaotic condition to reestablish their control over the Islas de la Bahía. As a result, Honduras wasted little time in formally seceding from the federation once it was free to do so. Independence was declared on November 15, 1838, and in January 1839, an independent constitution was formally adopted. Morazán then ruled only El Salvador, and in 1839 his forces there were attacked by a Honduran army commanded by General Francisco Ferrera. Ferrera was defeated but returned to attack again in the summer, only to suffer another defeat. The following year, Morazán himself was overthrown, and two years later he was shot in Costa Rica during a final, futile attempt to restore the United Provinces of Central America.

For Honduras, the first decades of independence were neither peaceful nor prosperous. The country's political turmoil attracted the ambitions of individuals and nations within and outside of Central America. Even geography contributed to its misfortunes. Alone among the Central American republics, Honduras had a border with the three potential rivals for regional hegemony Guatemala, El Salvador, and Nicaragua. This situation was exacerbated by the political division throughout the isthmus between liberals and conservatives. Any liberal or conservative regime saw a government of the opposite ideology on its borders as a potential threat. In addition, exiled opposition figures tended to gather in states whose governments shared their political affiliation and to use these states as launching pads for efforts to topple their own governments. For

15

the remainder of the century, Honduras's neighbors would constantly interfere in its internal politics.

After the fifteen-month interim presidency of Francisco Zelaya Ayes (1839-40), conservative General Ferrera became independent Honduras's first elected president. Ferrera's two-year term (1841- 42) was followed by a five-year period in which he alternately named himself president or allowed the congress to name an interim president while he maintained control of the country by holding the post then known as minister of war. Ferrera's last notable act was the unsuccessful attempt to depose the liberal Morazán as president of El Salvador. In 1847 Ferrera allowed fellow-conservative Juan Lindo Zelaya to assume the presidency. Under Lindo's presidency, a new constitution was adopted in 1848, and some effort was made to promote education, but any effort to make substantial improvements in the country's situation was doomed by continuing turmoil.

During Lindo's presidency (1847-52), the British began pressuring Honduras for the payment of debts and other claims. In 1849 a British naval force briefly occupied the port of Trujillo, destroying property and extorting 1,200 pesos from the local government. The following year, Lindo's own vice president revolted and was prevented from seizing power only through the military intervention of El Salvador and Nicaragua. All this turmoil may help to explain why Lindo refused an additional presidential term and instead turned over power in 1852 to the opposition liberals, headed by Trinidad Cabañas (1852-55). Three years later, the conservative government of Guatemala invaded Honduras and ousted Cabañas, installing in his place the conservative leader, Santos Guardiola.

The fighting between liberals and conservatives was temporarily set aside because of the 1855 appearance in Central America of an American soldier of fortune, William Walker, who established himself as president of Nicaragua in 1856. Cabañas briefly considered seeking Walker's aid in attempting to return to power. Instead, armies from all the countries of Central America joined to oppose Walker, who was forced to abandon Nicaragua in 1857 and return to the United States.

In 1859 the British agreed to a treaty that recognized Honduran sovereignty over the Islas de la Bahía. Some of the British settlers in the area objected to this transfer and appealed to Walker for help. Walker evidently thought that his return to Central America would be welcomed by the Honduran liberals, who were once again trying to oust Guardiola. Walker landed on the Honduran coast in 1860 but found little support and encountered determined opposition from both the Hondurans and the British. He surrendered to the British, who promptly handed him over to Honduran authorities. A few days later in 1860, he died in front of a Honduran firing squad.

The return of the Islas de la Bahía and the death of Walker ended the immediate threat to Honduran territorial integrity, but other Central American nations continued to be involved in Honduran internal affairs. Guardiola was assassinated by his own honor guard in 1862, and the following decade witnessed the presidency change hands almost twenty times. General José María Medina served as president or dictator eleven times during that period, but Guatemalan intervention in 1876 drove him and his conservative supporters from power.

From 1876 until 1882, liberal president Marco Aurelio Soto governed Honduras with the support of Guatemalan strongman General Justo Rufino Barrios. Soto succeeded not only in restoring order but also in implementing some basic reforms in finance, education, and public administration. But in 1883, he too fell into disfavor with Barrios and was forced to resign. His successor, General Luis Borgrán, survived in office until 1891 when General Poinciana Leiva (who had ruled briefly three times from 1873-76) was returned to power in a manipulated election. Although a liberal, Leiva tried to rule as an absolute dictator, dissolving the fledgling Liberal Party of Honduras (Partido Liberal de Honduras PLH) and deporting its leaders. The result was another round of civil conflict from which the reconstituted PLH ultimately emerged victorious. The PLH was led by Policarpo Bonilla, with the support of Nicaragua's liberal dictator, José Santos Zelaya.

When Bonilla assumed power in 1894, he began to restore a limited degree of order to the Honduran political scene. Another constitution was promulgated in 1895, and Bonilla was elected to a four-year term. Bonilla's administration revised civil codes, improved communications, and began an effort to resolve the long-standing boundary dispute with Nicaragua. Bonilla also ensured that in 1899, at the end of his term, he would be succeeded by his military commander, General Terencio Sierra.

The combined impact of civil strife and foreign interventions had doomed Honduras to a position of relative economic and social backwardness throughout the nineteenth century. The country had remained overwhelmingly rural; Tegucigalpa, Comayagua, and San Pedro Sula were the only towns of any size. In the early 1850s, the total population was estimated at 350,000, the overwhelming majority of whom were mestizos. By 1914 the population had grown to only 562,000.

Opportunities for education and culture were limited at best. Mid-nineteenth century records indicate that Honduras had no libraries and no regularly published newspapers. Two universities were maintained, although their quality was questionable. By the 1870s, only 275 schools, having approximately 9,000 pupils, existed in the entire country. In 1873-74, the government budgeted only the equivalent of US$720 for education, a sum designated for the national university.

Throughout the nineteenth century, Hondurans looked to mining as a means of improving their economic position. The mining industry had fallen into severe neglect in the first decades of the century, however. Many mines had been abandoned and flooded. During the years following independence, efforts to revive the industry were generally frustrating for both domestic and foreign entrepreneurs. Effort after effort was abandoned because of civil disturbances, lack of transportation, and poor health conditions.

Mining was revived somewhat in the 1880s. A key factor in this revival was the activity of the New York and Honduras Rosario Mining Company (NYHRMC), which had expanded rapidly and had become a major economic and political power within Honduras. Owing in part to the company's efforts, the Honduran government had allowed foreign mining companies to operate in Honduras with a minimum of restrictions and a virtual exemption from taxes. By 1889 the company was annually shipping bullion with a value of over US$700,000 to the United States. Profits from this operation were extremely high; the company's dividends for the first half of 1889 totaled US$150,000.

The NYHRMC's success attracted other companies to Honduras, and gold and silver exports became the principal source of foreign exchange for the rest of the century. The NYHRMC's success stood alone, however; most of the nearly 100 other companies were total failures. The Yuscarán Mining and Milling Company sold over US$5 million in stock but failed to begin effective production. By the end of the nineteenth century, the brief mining boom was in decline, although the NYHRMC would remain a major factor in the Honduran economy until the mid-twentieth century.

Although mining had provided foreign exchange, the vast majority of Hondurans gained their livelihoods from agriculture, usually on a subsistence level. Periodic efforts were made to develop agricultural exports, but they met with little success. Some tobacco, cattle, and hides were exported, mostly to neighboring countries. The recurring civil conflicts and the resultant confiscation of stock by various military commanders, however, put a damper on efforts to develop the cattle industry and contributed to its rather backward status. Some bananas and other fruits were exported from the Islas de la Bahía, much of this trade going to New Orleans, but the volume was small and the benefit for the rest of the nation almost imperceptible.

The Rise of United States Influence, 1899-1932

The Growth of the Banana Industry

Although the peaceful transfer of power from Bonilla to General Sierra in 1899 was important as the first time in decades that such a constitutional transition had taken place, that year was a watershed in another, even more important, sense. In 1889 the Vaccaro brothers of New Orleans, founders of what would become the Standard Fruit and Steamship Company (later known as Standard Fruit Company), shipped their first boatload of bananas from Honduras to New Orleans. The fruit found a ready market, and the trade grew rapidly. By 1902 local railroad lines were being constructed on the Caribbean coast to accommodate the expanding banana production.

Sierra's efforts to perpetuate himself in office led to his overthrow in 1903 by General Manuel Bonilla, who proved to be an even greater friend of the banana companies than Sierra had been. Companies gained exemptions from taxes and permission to construct wharves and roads, as well as permission to improve interior waterways and to obtain charters for new railroad construction.

Conservative Manuel Bonilla was an opponent rather than a relative or friend of Sierra's liberal predecessor, Policarpo Bonilla. During Manuel Bonilla's term in office, he imprisoned expresident Policarpo Bonilla for over two years and took other steps to suppress his political opposition, the liberals, who were the only group with an organized political party. The conservatives were divided into a host of personalist factions and lacked coherent leadership. Manuel Bonilla made some efforts to reorganize the conservatives into a "national party." The present-day National Party of Honduras

(Partido Nacional de Honduras PNH) traces its origins to his administration.

Manuel Bonilla promoted some internal improvements, notably road building. He improved the route from Tegucigalpa to the Pacific coast. On the international front, he concluded friendship pacts with Nicaragua and later with Guatemala and El Salvador.

Of perhaps greatest significance was the work accomplished during Manuel Bonillo's administration to delineate the longdisputed border with Nicaragua. The area, called the Mosquitia region, was located in the eastern part of the country in the department of Gracias a Dios. The area was large but virtually unpopulated except for small groups of Miskito who owed little allegiance to either nation. In 1894 a treaty provided for the establishment of a boundary commission, composed of representatives of Honduras and Nicaragua, to resolve the dispute. By 1904 the commission had been able to agree on only the lower part of the boundary. In that year, to reach agreement on the upper part, the representatives of the two nations picked King Alfonso XIII of Spain as a neutral, third member of the commission, in effect making him the arbiter. His decision, announced in 1906, gave the bulk of the disputed territory to Honduras, establishing the upper boundary line along the Río Coco. At the time, both governments accepted the decision, but in 1912 Nicaragua raised new objections. The dispute was finally resolved in favor of the 1906 arbitration only in 1960.

In 1906 Manuel Bonilla successfully resisted an invasion from Guatemala, but this was his last major success. The friendship pact with Guatemala and El Salvador signed in 1906 was interpreted as an anti-Nicaraguan alliance by the Nicaraguans. Nicaragua's powerful President Zelaya began to support exiled Honduran liberals in their efforts to topple Manuel Bonilla, who had become, in effect, the Honduran dictator. Supported by elements of the Nicaraguan army, the exiles invaded Honduras in February 1907 and established a provisional junta. With the assistance of Salvadoran troops, Manuel Bonilla tried to resist, but in March his forces were decisively beaten in a battle notable for the introduction of machine guns into Central American civil strife.

The Expanded Role of the United States

Until the early twentieth century, the United States had played only a very limited role in internal Honduran political clashes. Because there was not a resident United States minister in Tegucigalpa, the minister to Guatemala had been accredited for that position. The presence of the United States in the Caribbean increased following the Spanish-American War (1898), however. The decision to build a canal through Panama and expanded commercial activities led to a more active role for the United States government, as well as for United States companies.

By 1907 the United States looked with considerable disfavor on the role Zelaya of Nicaragua was playing in regional affairs. When the Nicaraguan army entered Honduras in 1907 to overthrow Bonilla, the United States government, believing that Zelaya wanted to dominate the entire region, landed marines at Puerto Cortés to protect the North American bananas trade. Other United States naval units prevented a Nicaraguan attack on Bonilla's last position at Amapala in the Golfo de Fonseca. After negotiations conducted by the United States naval commander, Manuel Bonilla sought refuge on the U.S.S. *Chicago*, and the fighting came to an end. The United States chargé d'affaires in Tegucigalpa took an active role in arranging a final peace settlement, with which Zelaya was less than happy. The settlement provided for the installation of a compromise regime, headed by General Miguel Dávila, in Tegucigalpa. Dávila was a liberal but was distrusted by Zelaya, who made a secret arrangement with El Salvador to oust him from office. This plan failed to reach fruition, but the United States, alarmed by the threat of renewed conflict in Central America, called the five Central American presidents to a conference in Washington in November.

The Central American Peace Conference of 1907 made a major effort to reduce the level of conflict within the region. A Honduran proposal to reestablish the political union of the Central American states failed to achieve acceptance, but several other measures were adopted. The five presidents signed the General Treaty of Peace and Amity of 1907 pledging themselves to establish the Permanent Central American Court of Justice, which would resolve future disputes. The treaty also committed the five countries to restrict the activities of exiles from neighboring states and provided the basis for legal extraditions. Of special interest was a United States-sponsored clause that provided for the permanent neutrality of Honduras in any future Central American conflicts. Another convention adopted by all five states committed the signers to withhold recognition from governments that seized power by revolutionary means. The United States and Mexico, which had acted as cosponsors of the conference, indicated informally that they would also deny recognition to such governments. From the point of view of the United States Department of State, these agreements represented a major step toward stabilizing Central America in general and Honduras in particular.

The first test of the new treaty involved Honduras. In 1908 opponents of President Dávila, probably supported by Guatemala and El Salvador, invaded the country. Nicaragua supported the Honduran president, and war seemed imminent. Perhaps motivated by the possibility of United States intervention, however, the parties agreed to submit the dispute to the new Central American court. The court ultimately rejected the Honduran and Nicaraguan complaints, but in the meantime the revolt collapsed, thus briefly restoring peace to Honduras.

Along with fighting off efforts to overthrow him, President Dávila made some attempts to modernize Honduras. He invited a Chilean officer to establish a regular military academy, which failed to survive beyond his time in office. Like his predecessor, Dávila encouraged the activities of the banana companies. The companies, however, were less than totally happy with him, viewing his administration as ineffective. In addition, rivalry among the companies became a factor in Honduran politics. In 1910 Dávila's administration granted the Vaccaro brothers a generous rail concession that included a provision prohibiting any rival line within twenty kilometers. This concession angered Samuel Zemurray of the newly formed Cuyamel Fruit Company. Zemurray had encouraged and even helped finance the 1908 invasion and was to continue to make trouble for the Dávila administration.

Despite the failure of the 1908 uprising, the United States remained concerned over Honduran instability. The administration of William Howard Taft saw the huge Honduran debt, over US$120 million, as a contributing factor to this instability and began efforts to refinance the largely British debt with provisions for a United States customs receivership or some similar arrangement. Negotiations were arranged between Honduran representatives and New York bankers, headed by J.P. Morgan. By the end of 1909, an agreement had been reached providing for a reduction in the debt and the issuance of new 5 percent bonds: the bankers would control the Honduran railroad, and the United States government would guarantee continued Honduran independence and would take control of customer revenue.

The terms proposed by the bankers met with considerable opposition in Honduras, further weakening the Dávila government. A treaty incorporating the key provisions was finally signed in January 1911 and submitted to the Honduran legislature by Dávila. However, that body, in a rare display of independence, rejected it by a vote of thirty-three to five.

An uprising in 1911 against Dávila interrupted efforts to deal with the debt problem. The United States stepped in to mediate the conflict, bringing both sides to a conference on one of its warships. The revolutionaries, headed by former president Manuel Bonilla, and the government agreed to a cease-fire and the installation of a provisional president who would be selected by the United States mediator, Thomas Dawson. Dawson selected Francisco Bertrand, who promised to hold early, free elections, and Dávila resigned. The 1912 elections were won by Manuel Bonilla, but he died after just over a year in office. Bertrand, who had been his vice president, returned to the presidency and in 1916 won election for a term that lasted until 1920.

The relative stability of the 1911-20 period was difficult to maintain. Revolutionary intrigues continued throughout the period, accompanied by constant rumors that one faction or another was being supported by one of the banana companies. Rivalry among these companies had escalated in 1910 when the United Fruit Company had entered Honduras. In 1913 United Fruit established the Tela Railroad Company and shortly thereafter a similar subsidiary, the Trujillo Railroad Company. The railroad companies were given huge land subsidies by the Honduran government for each kilometer of track they constructed. The government expected that in exchange for land the railroad companies would ultimately build a national rail system, providing the capital with its long-sought access to the Caribbean. The banana companies, however, had other ideas in mind. They used the railroads to open up new banana lands, rather than to reach existing cities. Through the resultant land subsidies, they soon came to control the overwhelming share of the best land along the Caribbean coast. Coastal cities such as La Ceiba, Tela, and Trujillo and towns further inland such as El Progreso and La Lima became virtual company towns, and the power of the companies often exceeded the authority wielded in the region by local governments.

For the next two decades, the United States government was involved in opposing Central American revolutions whether the revolutions were supported by foreign governments or by United States companies. During the 1912-21 period, warships were frequently dispatched to areas of revolutionary activity, both to protect United States interests and to exert a dampening effect on the revolutionaries. In 1917 the disputes among the companies threatened to involve Honduras in a war with Guatemala. The Cuyamel Fruit Company, supported by the Honduran government, had begun to extend its rail lines into disputed territory along the Guatemalan border. The Guatemalans, supported by the United Fruit Company, sent troops into the area, and it seemed for a time that war might break out. United States mediation ended the immediate threat, but the dispute smoldered until 1930 when a second United States mediation finally produced a settlement.

The development of the banana industry contributed to the beginnings of organized labor movements in Honduras and to the first major strikes in the nation's history. The first of these occurred in 1917 against the Cuyamel Fruit Company. The strike was suppressed by the Honduran military, but the following year additional labor disturbances occurred at the Standard Fruit Company's holding in La Ceiba. In 1920 a general strike hit the Caribbean coast. In response, a United States warship was dispatched to the area, and the Honduran government began arresting leaders. When Standard Fruit offered a new wage equivalent to US$1.75 per day, the strike ultimately collapsed. Labor troubles in the banana area, however, were far from ended.

World War I had a generally negative impact on Honduras. In 1914 banana prices began to fall, and, in addition, the war reduced the overall amount of agricultural exports. The United States entry into the war in 1917 diverted ships to the war effort, making imported goods, such as textiles scarce. The shortages of goods in turn led to inflation, and the decline in trade reduced government revenues from tariffs. The banana companies, however, continued to prosper; Standard Fruit reported earnings of nearly US$2.5 million in 1917. Despite its problems, Honduras supported the United States war effort and declared war on Germany in 1918.

The Threat of Renewed Instability, 1919-24

In 1919 it became obvious that Bertrand would refuse to allow an open election to choose his successor. Such a course of action was opposed by the United States and had little popular support in Honduras. The local military commander and governor of Tegucigalpa, General Rafael López Gutiérrez, took the lead in organizing PLH opposition to Bertrand. López Gutiérrez also solicited support from the liberal government of Guatemala and even from the conservative regime in Nicaragua. Bertrand, in turn, sought support from El Salvador. Determined to avoid an international conflict, the United States, after some hesitation, offered to meditate the dispute, hinting to the Honduran president that if he refused the offer, open intervention might follow. Bertrand promptly resigned and left the country. The United States ambassador helped arrange the installation of an interim government headed by Francisco Bográn, who promised to hold free elections. However, General López Gutiérrez, who now effectively controlled the military situation, made it clear that he was determined to be the next president. After considerable negotiation and some confusion, a formula was worked out under which elections were held. López Gutiérrez won easily in a manipulated election, and in October 1920 he assumed the presidency.

During Borgrán's brief time in office, he had agreed to a United States proposal to invite a United States financial adviser to Honduras. Arthur N. Young of the Department of State was selected for this task and began work in Honduras in August 1920, continuing to August 1921. While there, Young compiled extensive data and made numerous recommendations, even persuading the Hondurans to hire a New York police lieutenant to reorganize their police forces. Young's investigations clearly demonstrated the desperate need for major financial reforms in Honduras, whose always precarious budgetary situation was considerably worsened by the renewal of revolutionary activities. In 1919, for example, the military had spent more than double the amount budgeted for them, accounting for over 57 percent of all federal expenditures. Young's recommendations for reducing the military budget, however, found little favor with the new López Gutiérrez administration, and the government's financial condition remained a major problem. If anything, continued uprisings against the government and the threat of a renewed Central America conflict made the situation even worse. From 1919 to 1924, the Honduran government expended US$7.2 million beyond the amount covered by the regular budgets for military operations.

From 1920 through 1923, seventeen uprisings or attempted coups in Honduras contributed to growing United States concern over political instability in Central America. In August 1922, the presidents of Honduras, Nicaragua, and El Salvador met on the U.S.S. *Tacoma* in the Golfo de Fonseca. Under the watchful eye of the United States ambassadors to their nations, the presidents pledged to prevent their territories from being used to promote revolutions against their neighbors and issued a call for a general meeting of Central American states in Washington at the end of the year.

The Washington conference concluded in February with the adoption of the General Treaty of Peace and Amity of 1923, which had eleven supplemental conventions. The treaty in many ways followed the provisions of the 1907 treaty. The Central American court was reorganized, reducing the influence of the various governments over its membership. The clause providing for withholding recognition of revolutionary governments was expanded to preclude recognition of any revolutionary leader, his relatives, or anyone who had been in power six months before or after such an uprising unless the individual's claim to power had been ratified by free elections. The governments renewed their pledges to refrain from aiding revolutionary movements against their neighbors and to seek peaceful resolutions for all outstanding disputes.

The supplemental conventions covered everything from the promotion of agriculture to the limitation of armaments. One, which remained unratified, provided for free trade among all of the states except Costa Rica. The arms limitation agreement set a ceiling on the size of each nation's military forces (2,500 men for Honduras) and included a United States-sponsored pledge to seek foreign assistance in establishing more professional armed forces.

The October 1923 Honduran presidential elections and the subsequent political and military conflicts provided the first real tests of these new treaty arrangements. Under heavy pressure from Washington, López Gutiérrez allowed an unusually open campaign and election. The long-fragmented conservatives had reunited in the form of the National Party of Honduras (Partido Nacional de Honduras PNH), which ran as its candidate General Tiburcio Carías Andino, the governor of the department of Cortés. However, the liberal PLH was unable to unite around a single candidate and split into two dissident groups, one supporting former president Policarpo Bonilla, the other advancing the candidacy of Juan Angel Arias. As a result, each candidate failed to secure a majority. Carías received the greatest number of votes, with Bonilla second, and Arias a distant third. By the terms of the Honduran constitution, this stalemate left the final choice of president up to the legislature, but that body was unable to obtain a quorum and reach a decision.

In January 1924, López Gutiérrez announced his intention to remain in office until new elections could be held, but he repeatedly refused to specify a date for the elections. Carías, reportedly with the support of United Fruit, declared himself president, and an armed conflict broke out. In February the United States, warning that recognition would be withheld from anyone coming to power by revolutionary means, suspended relations with the López Gutiérrez government for its failure to hold elections.

Conditions rapidly deteriorated in the early months of 1924. On February 28, a pitched battle took place in La Ceiba between government troops and rebels. Even the presence of the U.S.S. *Denver* and the landing of a force of United States Marines were unable to prevent widespread looting and arson resulting in over US$2 million in property damage. Fifty people, including a United States citizen, were killed in the fighting. In the weeks that followed, additional vessels from the United States Navy Special Service Squadron were concentrated in Honduran waters, and landing parties were put ashore at various points to protect United States interests. One force of marines and sailors was even dispatched inland to Tegucigalpa to provide additional protection for the United States legation. Shortly before the arrival of the force, López Gutiérrez died, and what authority remained with the central government was being exercised by his cabinet. General Carías and a variety of other rebel leaders controlled most of the countryside but failed to coordinate their activities effectively enough to seize the capital.

In an effort to end the fighting, the United States government dispatched Sumner Welles to the port of Amapala; he had instructions to try to produce a settlement that would bring to power a government eligible for recognition under the terms of the 1923 treaty. Negotiations, which were once again held on board a United States cruiser, lasted from April 23 to April 28. An agreement was worked out that provided for an interim presidency headed by General Vicente Tosta, who agreed to appoint a cabinet representing all political factions and to convene a Constituent Assembly within ninety days to restore constitutional order. Presidential elections were to be held as soon as possible, and Tosta promised to refrain from being a candidate. Once in office, the new president showed signs of reneging on some of his pledges, especially those related to the appointment of a bipartisan cabinet. Under heavy pressure from the United States delegation, however, he ultimately complied with the provisions of the peace agreement.

Keeping the 1924 elections on track proved to be a difficult task. To put pressure on Tosta to conduct a fair election, the United States continued an embargo on arms to Honduras and barred the government from access to loans including a requested US$75,000 from the Banco Atlántida. Furthermore, the United States persuaded El Salvador, Guatemala, and Nicaragua to join in declaring that, under the 1923 treaty provision, no leader of the recent revolution would be recognized as president for the coming term. These pressures ultimately helped persuade Carías to withdraw his candidacy and also helped ensure the defeat of an uprising led by General Gregorio Ferrera of the PNH. The PNH nominated Miguel Paz Barahona (1925-29), a civilian, for president. The PLH, after some debate, refused to nominate a candidate, and on December 28 Paz Barahona won virtual unanimous election.

The Restoration of Order, 1925-31

Despite another minor uprising led by General Ferrera in 1925, Paz Barahona's administration was, by Honduran standards, rather tranquil. The banana companies continued to expand, the government's budgetary situation improved, and there was even an increase in labor organizing. On the international front, the Honduran government, after years of negotiations, finally concluded an agreement with the British bondholders to liquidate most of the immense national debt. The bonds were to be redeemed at 20 percent of face value over a thirty-year period. Back interest was forgiven, and new interest accrued only over the last fifteen years of this arrangement. Under the terms of this agreement, Honduras, at last, seemed on the road to fiscal solvency.

Fears of disturbances increased again in 1928 as the scheduled presidential elections approached. The ruling PNH nominated General Carías while the PLH, united again following the death of Policarpo Bonilla in 1926, nominated Vicente Mejía Colindres. To the surprise of most observers, both the campaign and the election were conducted with a minimum of violence and intimidation. Mejía Colindres won a decisive victory obtaining 62,000 votes to 47,000 for Carías. Even more surprising was Carías's public acceptance of defeat and his urging of his supporters to accept the new government.

Mejía Colindres took office in 1929 with high hopes for his administration and his nation. Honduras seemed on the road to political and economic progress. Banana exports, then accounting for 80 percent of all exports, continued to expand. By 1930 Honduras had become the world's leading producer of the fruit, accounting for one-third of the world's supply of bananas. United Fruit had come increasingly to dominate the trade, and in 1929 it bought out the Cuyamel Fruit Company, one of its two principal remaining rivals. Because conflicts between these companies had frequently led to support for rival groups in Honduran politics, had produced a border controversy with Guatemala, and may have even contributed to revolutionary disturbances, this merger seemed to promise greater domestic tranquility. The prospect for tranquility was further advanced in 1931 when Ferrera was killed while leading one last unsuccessful effort to overthrow the government.

Many of Mejía Colindres's hopes, however, were dashed with the onset of the Great Depression. Banana exports peaked in 1930, then declined rapidly. Thousands of workers were laid off, and the wages of those remaining on the job were reduced, as were the prices paid to independent banana producers by the giant fruit companies. Strikes and other labor disturbances began to break out in response to these conditions, but most were quickly suppressed with the aid of government troops. As the depression deepened, the government's financial situation deteriorated; in 1931 Mejía Colindres was forced to borrow US$250,000 from the fruit companies to ensure that the army would continue to be paid.

The Era of Tiburcio Carías Andino, 1932-54

Despite growing unrest and severe economic strains, the 1932 presidential elections in Honduras were relatively peaceful and fair. The peaceful transition of power was surprising because the onset of the depression had led to the overthrow of governments elsewhere throughout Latin America, in nations with much stronger democratic traditions than those of Honduras. Mejía Colindres, however, resisted pressure from his own party to manipulate the results to favor the PLH candidate, Angel Zúñiga Huete. As a result, the PNH candidate, Carías, won the election by a margin of some 20,000 votes. On November 16, 1932, Carías assumed office, beginning what was to be the longest period of continuous rule by an individual in Honduran history.

Lacking, however, was any immediate indication that the Carías administration was destined to survive any longer than most of its predecessors. Shortly before Carías's inauguration, dissident liberals, despite the opposition of Mejía Colindres, had risen in revolt. Carías had taken command of the government forces, obtained arms from El Salvador, and crushed the uprising in short order. Most of Carías's first term in office was devoted to efforts to avoid financial collapse, improve the military, engage in a limited program of road building, and lay the foundations for prolonging his own hold on power.

The economic situation remained extremely bad throughout the 1930s. In addition to the dramatic drop in banana exports caused by the depression, the fruit industry was further threatened by the outbreak in 1935 of epidemics of Panama disease (a debilitating fungus) and sigatoka (leaf blight) in the banana-producing areas. Within a year, most of the country's production was threatened. Large areas, including most of those around Trujillo, were abandoned, and thousands of Hondurans were thrown out of work. By 1937 a means of controlling the disease had been found, but many of the affected areas remained out of production because a significant share of the market formerly held by Honduras had shifted to other nations.

Carías had made efforts to improve the military even before he became president. Once in office, both his capacity and his motivation to continue and to expand such improvements increased. He gave special attention to the fledgling air force, founding the Military Aviation School in 1934 and arranging for a United States colonel to serve as its commandant.

As months passed, Carías moved slowly but steadily to strengthen his hold on power. He gained the support of the banana companies through opposition to strikes and other labor disturbances. He strengthened his position with domestic and foreign financial circles through conservative economic policies. Even in the height of the depression, he continued to make regular payments on the Honduran debt, adhering strictly to the terms of the arrangement with the British bondholders and also satisfying other creditors. Two small loans were paid off completely in 1935.

Political controls were instituted slowly under Carías. The Communist Party of Honduras (Partido Comunista de Honduras PCH) was outlawed, but the PLH continued to function, and even the leaders of a small uprising in 1935 were later offered free air transportation should they wish to return to Honduras from their exile abroad. At the end of 1935, however, stressing the need for peace and internal order, Carías began to crack down on the opposition press and political activities. Meanwhile, the PNH, at the president's direction, began a propaganda campaign stressing that only the continuance of Carías in office could give the nation continued peace and order. The constitution, however, prohibited immediate reelection of presidents.

The method chosen by Carías to extend his term of office was to call a constituent assembly that would write a new constitution and select the individual to serve for the first presidential term under that document. Except for the president's desire to perpetuate himself in office, there seemed little reason to alter the nation's basic charter. Earlier constituent assemblies had written thirteen constitutions (only ten of which had entered into force), and the latest had been adopted in 1924. The handpicked Constituent Assembly of 1936 incorporated thirty of the articles of the 1924 document into the 1936 constitution. The major changes were the elimination of the prohibition on immediate reelection of a president and vice president and the extension of the presidential term from four to six years. Other changes included restoration of the death penalty, reductions in the powers of the legislature, and denial of citizenship and therefore the right to vote to women. Finally, the new constitution included an article specifying that the incumbent president and vice president would remain in office until 1943. But Carías, by then a virtual dictator, wanted even more, so in 1939 the legislature, now completely controlled by the PNH, obediently extended his term in office by another six years (to 1949).

The PLH and other opponents of the government reacted to these changes by attempting to overthrow Carías. Numerous efforts were made in 1936 and 1937, but all were successful only in further weakening the PNH's opponents. By the end of the 1930s, the PNH was the only organized functioning political party in the nation. Numerous opposition leaders had been imprisoned, and some had reportedly been chained and put to work in the streets of Tegucigalpa. Others, including the leader of the PLH, Zúñiga Huete, had fled into exile.

During his presidency, Carías cultivated close relations with his fellow Central American dictators, generals Jorge Ubico in Guatemala, Maximiliano Hernández Martínez in El Salvador, and Anastasio Somoza García in Nicaragua. Relations were particularly close with Ubico, who helped Carías reorganize his secret police and also captured and shot the leader of a Honduran uprising who had made the mistake of crossing into Guatemalan territory. Relations with Nicaragua were somewhat more strained as a result of the continuing border dispute, but Carías and Somoza managed to keep this dispute under control throughout the 1930s and 1940s.

The value of these ties became somewhat questionable in 1944 when popular revolts in Guatemala and El Salvador deposed Ubico and Hernández Martínez. For a time, it seemed as if revolutionary contagion might spread to Honduras as well. A plot, involving some military officers as well as opposition civilians, had already been discovered and crushed in late 1943. In May 1944, a group of women began demonstrating outside of the Presidential Palace in Tegucigalpa, demanding the release of political prisoners.

Despite strong government measures, tension continued to grow, and Carías was ultimately forced to release some prisoners. This gesture failed to satisfy the opposition, and antigovernment demonstrations continued to spread. In July several demonstrators were killed by troops in San Pedro Sula. In October a group of exiles invaded Honduras from El Salvador but were unsuccessful in their efforts to topple the government. The military remained loyal, and Carías continued in office.

Anxious to curb further disorders in the region, the United States began to urge Carías to step aside and allow free elections when his current term in office expired. Carías, who by then was in his early seventies, ultimately yielded to these pressures and announced October 1948 elections, in which he would refrain from being a candidate. He continued, however, to find ways to use his power. The PNH nominated Carías's choice for president Juan Manuel Gálvez, who had been minister of war since 1933. Exiled opposition figures were allowed to return to Honduras, and the PLH, trying to overcome years of inactivity and division, nominated Zúñiga Huete, the same individual whom Carías had defeated in 1932. The PLH rapidly became convinced that it had no chance to win and, charging the government with manipulation of the electoral process, boycotted the elections. This act gave Gálvez a virtually unopposed victory, and in January 1949, he assumed the presidency.

Evaluating the Carías presidency is a difficult task. His tenure in office provided the nation with a badly needed period of relative peace and order. The country's fiscal situation improved steadily, education improved slightly, the road network expanded, and the armed forces were modernized. At the same time, nascent democratic institutions withered, opposition and labor activities were suppressed, and national interests at times were sacrificed to benefit supporters and relatives of Carías or major foreign interests.

Once in office, Gálvez demonstrated more independence than had generally been anticipated. Some policies of the Carías administration, such as road building and the development of coffee exports, were continued and expanded. By 1953 nearly one-quarter of the government's budget was devoted to road construction. Gálvez also continued most of the prior administration's fiscal policies, reducing the external debt and ultimately paying off the last of the British bonds. The fruit companies continued to receive favorable treatment at the hands of the Gálvez administration; for example, United Fruit received a highly favorable twenty-five-year contract in 1949.

Galvez, however, instituted some notable alterations from the preceding fifteen years. Education received increased attention and began to receive a larger share of the national budget. Congress actually passed an income tax law, although enforcement was sporadic at best. The most obvious change was in the political arena. A considerable degree of press freedom was restored, the PLH and other groups were allowed to organize, and even some labor organization was permitted. Labor also benefited from legislation during this period. Congress passed, and the president signed, legislation establishing the eight-hour workday, paid holidays for workers, limited employer responsibility for work-related injuries, and regulations for the employment of women and children.

Aborted Reform, 1954-63

The relative peace that Honduras had enjoyed for nearly two decades was shattered by a series of events during 1954, Gálvez's last year in office. Tension throughout the region had been increasing steadily as a confrontation developed between the left-leaning government of President Jacobo Arbenz Guzmán in Guatemala and the United States. Part of the confrontation involved the expropriation of United Fruit Company lands and charges that the Guatemalan government was encouraging agitation among the banana workers.

In 1952 the United States had begun considering actions to overthrow the Guatemalan government. Honduras had given asylum to several exiled opponents of Arbenz, including Colonel Carlos Castillo Armas, but Gálvez was reluctant to cooperate in direct actions against Guatemala, and the plans were not activated. By early 1954, however, a major covert operation against Guatemala was being organized, this time with greater Honduran cooperation. One reason for the cooperation was the Honduran government's concern over increased labor tensions in the banana-producing areas, tensions that the fruit companies blamed, in part, on Guatemalan influence.

Starting in early May 1954, the tensions escalated to strikes. First, a series of strikes broke out against United Fruit Company operations on Honduras's Caribbean coast. Within a few days, the strike spread to include the Standard Fruit Company operations, bringing the banana industry in the country to a near standstill. The strikers presented a wide range of grievances, involving wages, working conditions, medical benefits, overtime pay, and the right to collective bargaining. Initial government efforts to end the strike failed, and work stoppages began to spread into other industries. By May 21, the number of strikers was approaching 30,000, and the nation's economy was under severe strain.

As the strike was spreading, Honduras was also becoming more deeply involved in the movement to topple the Arbenz government in Guatemala. In late May, a military assistance agreement was concluded between the United States and Honduras, and large quantities of United States arms were quickly shipped to Honduras. Much of this incoming assistance was passed on to anti-Arbenz rebels commanded by Castillo Armas. In June these forces crossed into Guatemala and after several days of political maneuvering but little actual fighting, Arbenz fled into exile, and Castillo Armas became president. With the specter of foreign influence over the strike thus removed, negotiations began, and the strike ended in early July. Labor leaders who had been accused of having ties with Guatemala were jailed, and the final settlement, which met few of the original demands, was signed with elements more acceptable to the government and the fruit companies than to the workers. Despite the limited gains, however, the strike did mark a major step toward greater influence for organized labor in Honduras and a decline in the power of the fruit companies.

In the midst of these conflicts, the campaign for the 1954 elections continued. Unhappy with some of Gálvez's gestures toward liberalization, Carías, despite his advanced age, decided to run for president and secured the PNH nomination. This move, however, split the party, and more moderate members broke away to form the National Revolutionary Movement (Movimiento Nacional Revolucionario MNR). Their nominee was former vice president Abraham Williams Calderón. The split in the ruling party encouraged the PLH, who united behind Ramón Villeda Morales, a Tegucigalpa physician who was seen as somewhat to the left of center in the party's political spectrum.

Both the campaign and the election were remarkably free and honest. On October 10, 1954, approximately 260,000 out of over 400,000 eligible voters went to the polls. Villeda Morales won a large plurality with 121,213 votes, Carías received 77,041, and Williams carried 53,041. The PLH also gained a plurality in the legislature. Under Honduran law, however, a majority of the total votes was required to be elected president; Villeda Morales lacked a majority by just over 8,000 votes. The stage was set for a repeat of the confusing paralysis of 1924 because the constitution required, first, that two-thirds of the members of the new legislature must be present and vote to choose a president and, second, that the victor must receive two-thirds of the legislature's vote. To complicate matters further, Gálvez left for Miami reportedly to obtain medical treatment although some sources claim he merely fled the country, leaving the government in the hands of Vice President Julio Lozano Díaz.

Unable to reconcile their differences and unwilling to accept Villeda Morales as president, the PNH and MNR deputies boycotted the legislature, producing a national crisis. The constitution provided that in case of congressional deadlock the Supreme Court of Justice would select the president. Dominated as the court was by Carías appointees, the PLH opposed such a course of action. At this juncture, Lozano Díaz suddenly suspended the legislature and announced that he would act as president until new elections could be held. He declared that he would form a national government with cabinet members taken from all major parties and received pledges of support from all three candidates in the 1954 election. A Council of State, headed by a PLH member but including members of all three major parties, was appointed to replace the suspended congress until a constituent assembly could be chosen to write yet another constitution.

Lozano Díaz began his period as president with a broad base of support that eroded rapidly. He unveiled an ambitious development plan to be financed by international loans and increased taxes and also introduced the nation's first labor code. This document guaranteed workers the right to organize and strike but gave employers the right of lockout and forbade strikes in public services. The code also embodied some social welfare and minimum- wage provisions and regulated hours and working conditions. All these provisions gained him some labor support, but in later months relations between the president and labor began to sour.

As time passed, it became clear that Lozano Díaz had ambitions to replace the traditional parties with one that he controlled and could use to help prolong his hold on power. He reduced the Council of State to a consultative body, postponed elections, and set about forming his own party, the National Unity Party (Partido de Unidad Nacional PUN). The activities of other parties were limited, and, in July 1956, Villeda Morales and other PLH leaders were suddenly arrested and flown into exile. A few weeks later, the government crushed an uprising by 400 troops in the capital. Public opinion, however, was becoming increasingly hostile to the president, and rumors of his imminent fall had begun to circulate.

Following the August 1956 uprising, Lozano Díaz's health began to deteriorate, but he clung stubbornly to power. Elections for the legislature in October were boycotted by most of the opposition, who charged that the process was openly rigged to favor the president's supporters. The results seemed to confirm this charge, as the PUN candidates were declared the winners of all fifty-six seats in the congress. The joy of their victories was short, however. On October 21, the armed forces, led by the commanders of the army and air force academies and by Major Roberto Gálvez, the son of the former president, ousted Lozano Díaz and set up a military junta to rule the country.

This coup marked a turning point in Honduran history. For the first time, the armed forces had acted as an institution rather than as the instrument of a political party or of an individual leader. The new rulers represented younger, more nationalistic, and reform-minded elements in the military. They were products of the increased professionalization of the 1940s and 1950s. Most had received some training by United States military advisers, either in Honduras or abroad. For decades to come, the military would act as the final arbiter of Honduran politics.

The military's largest problem was the holding of elections for a legislature and the selection of a new president. A system of proportional representation was agreed upon, and elections were held in October. The PLH won a majority, and in November, by a vote of thirty-seven to twenty, the assembly selected Villeda Morales as president for a six-year term beginning January 1, 1958.

The new PLH administration undertook several major efforts to improve and modernize Honduran life. Funds were obtained from the International Monetary Fund (IMF) to stabilize the currency and from the World Bank to begin paving a highway from the Caribbean coast to the capital. Other efforts were undertaken to expand education. The greatest attention was devoted to passing a new labor code, establishing a social security system, and beginning a program of agrarian reform.

The reform program produced increasing opposition among the more conservative elements in Honduran society. There were scattered uprisings during Villeda Morales's initial years in power, but the military remained loyal and quickly crushed the disturbances. Military support began to evaporate in the early 1960s, however. Waning military support was in part a result of rising criticism of the government by conservative organizations such as the National Federation of Agriculturists and Stockraisers of Honduras (Federación Nacional de Agricultores y Ganaderos de Honduras Fenagh), which represented the large landowners. The shift in the military's attitude also reflected concern over what were viewed as more frequent rural disorder and growing radical influences in labor and peasant groups. Deteriorating relations with neighboring states, notably Nicaragua, also contributed to the tension. The major causes of friction, however, were the president's 1957 creation of the Civil Guard (Guardia Civil) a militarized police commanded directly by the president rather than the chief of the armed forces and the prospect of another PLH victory in the 1963 elections.

The elections were scheduled for October 1963. As in 1954, the PLH was confronting a divided opposition. The PNH nominated Ramón Ernesto Cruz, but a faction split off and ran the son of ex-president Carías. The PLH ignored the wishes of their president and nominated Modesto Rodas Alvarado, a charismatic, highly partisan figure believed to be to the left of Villeda Morales. All signs pointed to an overwhelming victory for the PLH, an outcome that the military found increasingly unpalatable.

Rumors of a coup began circulating in late summer of 1963. The United States endeavored to make clear its opposition to such action even dispatching a high-ranking officer from the United States Southern Command in the Panama Canal Zone to try to convince the chief of the armed forces, Air Force Colonel Oswaldo López Arellano, to call off the coup. Villeda Morales also tried to calm military fears, taking the carbines away from the Civil Guard and opposing plans for a constitutional amendment to restore direct command of the military to the president. All these efforts failed, however. Before dawn on October 3, 1963, the military moved to seize power. The president and the PLH's 1963 presidential candidates were flown into exile, Congress was dissolved, the constitution was suspended, and the planned elections were canceled. Colonel López Arellano proclaimed himself president, and the United States promptly broke diplomatic relations.

Military Rule and International Conflict, 1963-78

López Arellano rapidly moved to consolidate his hold on power. Growing radical influence had been one of the reasons advanced to justify the coup; once in power the government disbanded or otherwise attacked communist, pro-Castro, and other elements on the left. The Agrarian Reform Law was effectively nullified, in part by the regime's refusal to appropriate money for the National Agrarian Institute (Instituto Nacional Agrario INA). The country's two peasant unions were harassed, although a new organization of rural workers, the National Union of Peasants (Unión Nacional de Campensinos UNC), which had Christian Democratic ties, actually expanded in the mid- and late-1960s. López Arellano promised to call elections for yet another legislature, and early in 1964 his government was recognized by the new United States administration of President Lyndon B. Johnson. Shortly thereafter, military assistance, which had been suspended following the coup, was resumed.

Close ties soon developed between the military government and the PNH. A key factor in the development of these links was PNH leader Ricardo Zúñiga Augustinius, who became secretary of state for the presidency, the key cabinet position. Numerous other party members served in the government, giving it a civil-military character but widening the gap between the administration and the PLH. Also linked to the government was a secret organization used to attack the left and intimidate political opponents. Known as the Mancha Brava (Tough Spot), it reputedly drew much of its membership from the ranks of public employees.

To give a semblance of legality to his government, López Arellano promulgated a new constitution with a unicameral Congress. He then called elections for this new Congress. A general amnesty for political figure was decreed in November, exiles were allowed to return, and the PLH resumed political activity. The PNH had pledged throughout the campaign that if it gained control of the Congress, its members would select López Arellano as president. The vote was held on February 16, 1965; the PNH won 35 seats, the PLH 29. The PLH charged the government with fraudulently manipulating the results, and some party leaders urged their supporters to boycott meetings of the assembly. The PLH was unable to agree on this tactic, and enough PLH members took their seats when the Congress convened on March 15 to provide the necessary quorum. The PNH delegates kept their promise and elected López Arellano as president for a new six-year term, from 1965 to 1971.

For a time, López Arellano had success in foreign affairs. One of his government's first acts had been to join with Guatemala and Nicaragua in establishing the Central American Defense Council (Consejo de Defensa Centroamericana Condeca), which was a military pact among these Central American states and the United States for coordination of counterinsurgency activities. El Salvador joined shortly thereafter, and in 1965 Condeca held its first joint military exercise on the Caribbean coast of Honduras. That same year, Honduras contributed a small contingent of troops to the Organization of American States (OAS) forces monitoring the election in the Dominican Republic.

As the 1960s progressed, Honduras's relations with Nicaragua and with the United States improved, but increasing problems developed between Honduras and El Salvador. In May and June 1967, a series of incidents along the border aggravated tensions considerably. One incident involved the capture of two Salvadoran officers and thirty-nine enlisted men whose truck convoy had penetrated several kilometers into Honduras. The Salvadoran troops were finally returned over a year later, but the tensions continued to mount.

War with El Salvador

By 1968 the López Arellano regime seemed to be in serious trouble. The economic situation was producing growing labor conflicts, political unrest, and even criticism from conservative groups such as Fenagh. Municipal elections were held in March 1968 to the accompaniment of violence and charges of open fraud, producing PNH victories but also fueling public discontent and raising the concern of the United States Embassy. Efforts at opening up a dialogue were made in mid-1968 but had little success. Later in the year a general strike was kept brief by government action that helped break the strike and exiled the leader of the major Caribbean coast labor federation. Unrest continued, however; in the spring of 1969 new strikes broke out among teachers and other groups.

As the political situation deteriorated, the Honduran government and some private groups came increasingly to place blame for the nation's economic problems on the approximately 300,000 undocumented Salvadoran immigrants in Honduras. Fenagh began to associate Salvadoran immigrants with illegal land invasions, and in January 1969, the Honduran government refused to renew the 1967 Bilateral Treaty on Immigration with El Salvador that had been designed to regulate the flow of individuals across their common border. In April INA announced that it would begin to expel from their lands those who had acquired property under agrarian reform without fulfilling the legal requirement that they be Honduran by birth. Attacks were also launched in the media on the impact of Salvadoran immigrant labor on unemployment and wages on the Caribbean coast. By late May, Salvadorans began to stream out of Honduras back to an overpopulated El Salvador.

Tensions continued to mount during June 1969. The soccer teams of the two nations were engaged that month in a three-game elimination match as a preliminary to the World Cup. Disturbances broke out during the first game in Tegucigalpa, but the situation got considerably worse during the second match in San Salvador. Honduran fans were roughed up, the Honduran flag and national anthem were insulted, and the emotions of both nations became considerably agitated. Actions against Salvadoran residents in Honduras, including several vice consuls, became increasingly violent. An unknown number of Salvadorans were killed or brutalized, and tens of thousands began fleeing the country. The press of both nations contributed to a growing climate of near-hysteria, and on June 27, 1969, Honduras broke diplomatic relations with El Salvador.

Early on the morning of July 14, 1969, concerted military action began in what came to be known as the Soccer War. The Salvadoran air force attacked targets inside Honduras and the Salvadoran army launched major offensives along the main road connecting the two nations and against the Honduran islands in the Golfo de Fonseca. At first, the Salvadorans made fairly rapid progress. By the evening of July 15, the Salvadoran army, which was considerably larger and better equipped than its Honduran opponent, pushed the Honduran army back over eight kilometers and captured the departmental capital of Nueva Ocotepeque. Thereafter, the attack bogged down, and the Salvadorans began to experience fuel and ammunition shortages. A major reason for the fuel shortage was the action of the Honduran air force, which in addition to largely destroying the smaller Salvadoran air force had severely damaged El Salvador's oil storage facilities.

The day after the fighting had begun, the OAS met in an urgent session and called for an immediate cease-fire and a withdrawal of El Salvador's forces from Honduras. El Salvador resisted the pressures from the OAS for several days, demanding that Honduras first agree to pay reparations for the attacks on Salvadoran citizens and guarantee the safety of those Salvadorans remaining in Honduras. A cease-fire was arranged on the night of July 18; it took full effect only on July 20. El Salvador continued until July 29 to resist pressures to withdraw its troops. Then a combination of pressures led El Salvador to agree to a withdrawal in the first days of August. Those persuasive pressures included the possibility of OAS economic sanctions against El Salvador and the dispatch of OAS observers to Honduras to oversee the security of Salvadorans remaining in that country. The actual war had lasted just over four days, but it would take more than a decade to arrive at a final peace settlement.

The war produced only losses for both sides. Between 60,000 and 130,000 Salvadorans had been forcibly expelled or had fled from Honduras, producing serious economic disruption in some areas. Trade between the two nations had been totally disrupted and the border closed, damaging the economies of both nations and threatening the future of the Central American Common Market (CACM). Up to 2,000 people, the majority Honduran civilians, had been killed, and thousands of other Hondurans in the border area had been made homeless. Airline service between the two nations was also disrupted for over a decade.

After the war, public support for the military plummeted. Although the air force had performed well, the army had not. Criticism of the army was not limited to the public; junior officers were often vocal in their criticism of superiors, and a rift developed between junior and senior officers.

The war, however, led to a new sense of Honduran nationalism and national pride. Tens of thousands of Honduran workers and peasants had gone to the government to beg for arms to defend their nation. Local defense committees had sprung up, with thousands of ordinary citizens, often armed only with machetes, taking over local security duties. This response to the fighting made a strong impression on a sector of the officer corps and contributed to an increased concern over national development and social welfare among the armed forces.

The internal political struggle had been briefly suspended during the conflict with El Salvador, but by the start of 1970 it was again in full swing. The government was under pressure to initiate administrative and electoral reforms, allow open elections in 1971, reorganize the military, and adopt new economic programs, including a revision of Honduran relations with the CACM. Labor, peasant, and business organizations were meeting together in what were known as the *fuerzas vivas* (living forces). Their representatives met with López Arellano and proposed a Plan of National Unity, calling for free elections, a coalition cabinet, and a division of government posts and congressional seats. These proposals failed to elicit immediate response, but discussions continued. Meanwhile, a general political amnesty was decreed, the creation of the Honduran Christian Democratic Party (Partido Demócrata Cristiano de Honduras PDCH) was announced, and a decree was issued calling for presidential and congressional elections on March 28, 1971.

After considerable discussion and debate, the PHL and PNH parties responded to pressures from labor, business, and the military. On January 7, 1971, they signed a political pact agreeing to establish a national-unity government after the March elections. The purposes of the pact were twofold. The first was to present a single slate of congressional candidates that would divide the Congress equally between the PLH and PNH (each party would run its own candidate for the presidency, however.) The second goal was to promote the Minimum Government Plan (Plan Mínimo de Gobierno), which included achieving agrarian reform, increasing technical education, passing a civil service law, attempting to resolve the conflict with El

Salvador, restructuring the CACM, and reforming government administration. A later agreement between the parties the "little pact" ("pactito") agreed to a division of government posts, including those in the Supreme Court of Justice.

The 1971 elections were relatively free and honest. Both parties offered presidential candidates who were compromise choices of the major party factions. The PLH ran Jorge Bueso Arias, and the PNH nominated Ramón Ernesto Cruz. Most observers anticipated a PLH victory, but the PNH ran a more aggressive campaign, making use of the mass media and of modern campaign techniques for the first time in Honduran history. On election day, Cruz scored an impressive victory, gaining 299,807 votes to 269,989 for Bueso Arias. However, a disturbing note for the PNH was that popular participation in the election had declined significantly from 1965. Only slightly over two-thirds of those registered to vote had done so, although the constitution made voting obligatory.

At first, Cruz appeared to be living up to the terms of the agreements between the parties. He appointed five PLH members, five PNH members, and one military officer to his cabinet. López Arellano remained as chief of the armed forces. As time passed, however, the split between PLH and PNH widened steadily. In order to deal with the budget crisis, Cruz pushed through a reluctant Congress a bill that cut tax benefits and import exemptions. This bill produced opposition from both business and labor sectors. In the area of agrarian reform, the president soon removed INA's dynamic director, Roberto Sandoval, and replaced him with a PNH member, Horacio Moya Posas, who slowed the pace of reform. The PLH protested this action and also argued that the appointment of PNH supporters to the Supreme Court of Justice violated the agreement. Finally, in March 1972, the president dismissed two of the PLH cabinet members. By mid-1972, the government had lost most of its non-PNH support.

Military Rule and Reform

During the autumn of 1972, with the support of the military, the two parties attempted to revise the arrangements between the parties and the major labor and business groups. These efforts were not unsuccessful, and opposition to what was increasingly perceived as an ineffectual and divisive administration spread steadily. The virtual halting of agrarian reform and the killing of several peasants by the military in the department of Olancho had angered peasant groups. Labor and business were alienated by the ineffective efforts to deal with the problems of the economy. The PLH felt that its position within the government was steadily eroding and that its agreement with the PNH was regularly violated. In December peasant and labor organizations announced a hunger march by 20,000 individuals to Tegucigalpa to protest the government's agrarian policies. Supported by a prior agreement with the labor movement, the military on December 4, 1972, overthrew Cruz in a bloodless coup and once again installed López Arellano as the president.

Problems for the López Arellano regime began to increase in 1974. The economy was still growing at a slow pace, partly because of the immense damage caused to the Caribbean coast by Hurricane Fifi in September 1974. The storm was the most devastating natural disaster in recent Honduran history, claiming 10,000 or more lives and destroying a vast number of banana plants. The disaster also increased calls for agrarian reform.

The government's greatest problem, however, centered on another aspect of the banana industry. Honduras had joined other bananaexporting nations in a joint agreement to levy an export tax on that fruit. The Honduran tax had taken effect in April 1974 but was suddenly canceled four months later. Shortly thereafter, reports began to circulate that the United Fruit Company had paid more than US$1 million to Honduran officials to secure the repeal of the tax. Prominently implicated in these accusations were López Arellano and his minister of economy and commerce.

Reacting to these charges on March 31, 1975, the military relieved López Arellano of his position as chief of the armed forces, replacing him with Colonel Juan Alberto Melgar Castro. Just over three weeks later, they completed the process by removing López Arellano from the presidency and replacing him with Melgar Castro. These decisions had been made by the increasingly powerful Supreme Council of the Armed Forces (Consejo Superior de las Fuerzas Armadas Consuffaa), a group of approximately twenty to twenty-five key colonels of the armed forces who provided the institution with a form of collective leadership.

In July 1976 the border with El Salvador was still disputed. In July a minor upsurge of conflict there brought prompt OAS intervention, which helped to keep the conflict from escalating. In October both nations agreed to submit their dispute to arbitration. This development raised hopes for a rapid peace settlement. Progress, however, proved slow; and tensions were raised again, briefly, in 1978, when the Honduran government abruptly canceled all permits for travel to El Salvador. The rise of guerrilla conflict in El Salvador, plus strong pressures from other nations, made a settlement increasingly urgent in subsequent months. In October 1980, with Peruvian mediation, the bilateral General Peace Treaty was finally signed in Lima, Peru. Trade and travel were soon resumed, but numerous problems, including final adjudication of some small parcels of territory along the frontier, remained for later consideration.

Relations with Nicaragua had also become more difficult, especially after civil conflict had increased in that nation in the late 1970s. In March 1978, Honduran soldiers captured Germán Pomares, a leader of the Sandinista National Liberation Front (Frente Sandinista de Liberación Nacional FSLN), the guerrilla force fighting against the regime of Anastasio Somoza Debayle in Nicaragua. Pomares was held until the end of June, but Nicaraguan requests for extradition were denied, and he was ultimately flown to Panama. As fighting in Nicaragua escalated in 1978 and early 1979,

Honduras found itself in a difficult position. Honduras did not want to support the unpopular Somoza regime but feared the Marxist leanings of the FSLN. In addition, beginning in September 1978, Honduras had become burdened with an ever-growing number of refugees from Nicaragua.

The Return to Civilian Rule, 1978-82

Melgar Castro's hold on power began to dissolve in 1978. Charges of government corruption and of military links with narcotics traffic had become increasingly widespread, leading to accusations that the government had failed to adequately defend the country. Melgar's hold on power had weakened because he lacked support among large landowners. In addition, the Melgar government had seemed to be making little progress toward promised elections, leading to suspicions that it hoped to prolong its time in office. Right-wing political forces criticized the Melgar administration's handling of the Ferrari Case, which involved drug trafficking and murder of civilians and in which members of the military had been implicated. Unions and student organizations correctly interpreted the rightwing 's criticism as a prelude to a coup. When demonstrators took to the streets to support Melgar, right-wing elements within the military charged Melgar had lost control of public order and ousted him. On August 7, 1978, Melgar Castro and his cabinet were replaced by a three-member junta. Led by General Policarpo Paz García, chief of the armed forces, and including the air force commander and the chief of military security, the junta had close ties to the large landowners and moved to protect the military men involved in the Ferrari Case.

From its inception, the government of Paz García had promised to return Honduras to civilian rule. In April 1980, the Honduran citizenry was summoned to the polls to choose delegates for a new Congress. The Congress would select an interim government and would establish procedures for presidential and congressional elections in 1981.

Early indications for the 1980 elections pointed toward a victory for the PNH, headed by Ricardo Zúñiga. The PNH appeared more unified and organized than the rival PLH, and most people assumed that the PNH would be favored by the ruling military. The PLH suffered from internal divisions and a lack of leadership. Former president Villeda Morales had died in 1971, and the party's leader after his death, Modesto Rodas Alvarado, had died in 1979. A split had developed between the more conservative followers of Rodas and the party's left wing, which had formed the Popular Liberal Alliance (Alianza Liberal del Pueblo Alipo). In addition, a third party, the Innovation and Unity Party (Partido de Inovación y Unidad Pinu) had been registered and was expected to draw support away from the PLH. The PNH had succeeded in blocking the inscription of the PDCH, leading the PDCH adherents to join with groups further to the left in denouncing the elections as a farce and a fraud and urging popular abstention.

The April 1980 election produced a record registration and voter turnout. More than 1.2 million Hondurans registered, and over 1 million voted over 81 percent of those eligible. The high number of voters evidently favored the PLH, which won 49.4 percent of the votes cast. Under a complex apportionment system, the PLH won thirty-five seats in the Congress; the PNH, thirty-three; and Pinu, three. This result produced considerable debate over the composition of the next government. There was general agreement on naming Paz García as interim president, and the disputes centered on the composition of the cabinet. Ultimately, a PLH leader, Roberto Suazo Córdova, was made president of the Congress, while the PLH also gained five of the seats on the new Supreme Court of Justice. The cabinet was divided among all three parties and the military; the armed forces received the Ministry of National Defense and Public Security, as well as the Ministry of Foreign Affairs, and the PNH acquired key economic positions.

The Congress took more than a year to draft a new constitution and an electoral law for the 1981 presidential and congressional elections. The work went slowly, and the elections originally scheduled for August 1981 had to be postponed until November. In the interim, the National Elections Tribunal (Tribunal Nacional de Elecciones TNE) unanimously granted the PDCH the legal status needed for a place on the 1981 ballot.

Despite the presence of candidates for the Pinu and the PDCH on the November 1981 ballot, it was clear that the election would be essentially a two-party affair between the PLH and PNH. On November 29, 1981, a total of 1,214,735 Hondurans, 80.7 percent of those registered, voted, giving the PLH a sweeping victory. Suazo Córdova won 636,392 votes (52.4 percent), the PNH 491,089 votes, and 48,582 votes were divided between the Pinu and the PDCH. The PLH also took control of Congress, winning forty-four seats; the PNH, thirtyfour ; the Pinu, three; and the PDCH, one. The PLH also won 61 percent of the municipal councils. Suazo Córdova was inaugurated as president of Honduras in January 1982, ending nearly a decade of military presidents.

United States and the Central American Crisis

President Suazo Córdova assumed office at a time of extreme political ferment in Central America. The United States government was seeking to halt or roll back the advances of what it considered to be pro-Soviet forces on the isthmus. The leftist insurgency launched by the Farabundo Martí National Liberation Front (Frente Farabundo Martí de Liberación Nacional FMLN) in El Salvador had been underway for some two years, and the outcome of the struggle in that country was in doubt. In Nicaragua, the FSLN with close ties to Cuba, the Soviet Union, and other communist states ruled repressively and continued a military buildup unprecedented for the region. Honduras a country poor in resources, lacking in democratic traditions, and strategically located between these two revolutionary governments almost inexorably drew the attention and involvement of Washington.

The Suazo Córdova Administration

Suazo Córdova, a country doctor from La Paz, was a veteran of Honduran political infighting, but he lacked the kind of experience that might have prepared him for the internationalist role he would play as president of the republic. His initial approach to the question of Honduras's role in the growing regional crisis appeared to stress coexistence rather than confrontation. This approach reflected Honduras's historical passivity in regional and international affairs and took into account the regional balance of power, which did not favor Honduras. As a result, Suazo Córdova's inaugural speech stressed the issues of self-determination and the administration's desire to remain neutral in the face of regional upheaval.

In keeping with this conciliatory approach, on March 23, 1982, Minister of Foreign Affairs Edgardo Paz Barnica proposed a peace plan to the permanent council of the OAS. The plan was based on the following six points: general disarmament in Central America, the reduction of foreign military and other advisers (then a real point of contention with the Nicaraguan government), international supervision of any final agreement, an end to regional arms traffic, respect for delineated and demarcated borders, and the establishment of a permanent multilateral dialogue. The proposal met with little support from other Central American states, particularly Nicaragua.

Gradually, the Suazo Córdova administration began to perceive the FSLN (commonly referred to as Sandinista) administration as obstructionist in regional and international forums, as well as a subversive force that intended to undermine political stability in Honduras through intimidation, propaganda, and direct aid to incipient insurgent groups. The emergence of a consensus on this point within both the Honduran administration and armed forces coincided with a significant expansion of the United States role in Honduras, both as policy adviser and as purveyor of military and economic aid.

Brigadier General Gustavo Álvarez Martínez, who assumed the position of commander of the armed forces in January 1982 emerged as a hardliner against the Sandinistas. Álvarez publicly declared Honduras "in a war to the death" with Nicaragua; he believed such a war should be conducted under the auspices of a triple alliance among Guatemala, El Salvador, and Honduras. Some observers also believed that Álvarez had another aspect to his anticommunist strategy, namely covert domestic surveillance and extralegal executions. Álvarez's training in Argentina, where such "dirty war" tactics were common in the 1970s, lent some credence to the charges of increased disappearances and other less extreme forms of harassment against the Honduran left. Álvarez's main rival for the post of armed forces commander, Colonel Leónidas Torres Arias, the former head of military intelligence, had assumed an attaché post in Buenos Aires, Argentina, after losing the struggle for command. From Argentina, Torres proceeded to castigate Álvarez in the media, charging that the general operated a personal death squad. The Honduran Committee for the Defense of Human Rights appeared to confirm Torres's charges to some degree by reporting an increase in the number of political disappearances nationwide. According to foreign observers, the total numbers in no way rivaled those registered in El Salvador or Guatemala; the increase, however, was statistically significant for previously tranquil Honduras.

Álvarez's strong-arm tactics drew criticism from some observers, particularly the foreign press and international human rights groups. At the same time, however, leftist subversive activity did expand in the early 1980s. Much of this increase was attributed directly or indirectly to Sandinista support for like-minded Honduran groups such as the PCH, the Lorenzo Zelaya Popular Revolutionary

Forces (Fuerzas Populares Revolucionarias-Lorenzo Zelaya FPR-LZ), and the Honduran Revolutionary Party of Central American Workers (Partido Revolucionario de los Trabajadores Centroamericanos de Honduras PRTC-H). Beginning with minor bombings, these groups eventually progressed to kidnappings and hijackings. The most ambitious effort was that launched by a platoon-sized unit of Nicaraguan-trained PRTC-H members who crossed the border from Nicaragua into Olancho department in September 1983. A rapid response by Honduran troops isolated the PRTC-H column; twenty- three of the guerrillas surrendered, and another twenty-six died in the mountains, many of starvation and exposure. A similar incursion in 1984 also failed to strike a revolutionary spark among the conservative Honduran peasantry.

The perception of a genuine leftist revolutionary threat to Honduran stability enhanced Brigadier General Álvarez's power and heightened his profile both in Honduras and the United States. The resultant appearance of an imbalance of power between the military and the nascent civilian government called into question the viability of Honduras's democratic transition. Some observers saw in Álvarez a continuation in the long series of military caudillos who had ruled the nation since independence. A coup and reimposition of direct military rule appeared a virtual certainty to those who doubted Honduras's affinity for any form of democratic government. Others, however, pictured Álvarez more in the mold of Argentina's Juan Perón a military-based caudillo who successfully made the transition to populist civilian politics. Like most officers, Álvarez had ties to the PNH. Álvarez served as president of the Association for the Progress of Honduras (Asociación para el Progreso de Honduras Aproh), a group made up mainly of conservative businesspeople and PNH leaders. The initial goals of Aproh were to attract foreign investment and to block the growth of "popular organizations" (labor unions, campesino groups, and other activist groups) such as those that supported the FMLN in El Salvador. Aproh's acceptance of funding from the South Korea-based Unification Church proved controversial and generated negative publicity for both the organization and for Álvarez. The general's purportedly popular following, moreover, was suspect. He seemed much more comfortable and adept at high-level political maneuvering than at grassroots organization. Eventually, even his support within the armed forces proved to be inadequate to sustain his ambitions.

Although Álvarez had appeared ascendant by 1982, some observers described the political situation in Honduras as a triumvirate: Brigadier General Álvarez formulating national security policy and refraining from a direct military takeover of the government; President Suazo supporting Álvarez's policies in return for military tolerance of his rule and military support for his domestic policies; and the United States government providing the economic and military aid that helped sustain the arrangement. Some disputed the claim that Suazo was subservient to the military by pointing out the fact that the president refused to increase the budget of the armed forces. That budget, however, failed to take foreign military aid into account. The increase in United States military aid from US$3.3 million in fiscal year (FY) 1980 to US$31.3 million in FY 1982, therefore, represented a substantial expansion in the military's role in government.

Álvarez strongly supported United States policy in Central America. He reportedly assisted in the initial formation of the Nicaraguan Resistance (more commonly known as the Contras, short for *contrarevolucionarios* counterrevolutionaries in Spanish), arranged large-scale joint exercises with United States forces, and agreed to allow the training of Salvadoran troops by United States special forces at a facility near Puerto Castilla known as the Regional Center for Military Training (Centro Regional de Entrenamiento Militar CREM). The latter action eventually contributed greatly to Álvarez's ouster in early 1984.

The other major factor in the Álvarez ouster was the general's attempt to streamline the command structure of the armed forces. Traditionally, a collegial board made up of field-grade officers consulted with the commander in the formulation of policy for the

Honduran armed forces. Álvarez proposed to eliminate this organization, the Supreme Council of the Armed Forces (Consejo Superior de las Fuerzas Armadas Consuffaa), and to replace it with a board of eight senior officers. The reorganization would have concentrated and enhanced Álvarez's power over the military by allowing him to name his most trusted commanders to a leadership board that would rubber-stamp his policy proposals. At the same time, the reorganization had promised to make the armed forces function more efficiently, an important consideration if hostilities broke out between Honduras and Nicaragua.

Alvarez's view on involvement in Nicaragua led directly to the 1984 rebellion by his officers. Most observers had expected Honduras to serve as one staging area for a United States military intervention in Nicaragua if such an operation took place. The flawed but successful Operation Urgent Fury on the Caribbean island of Grenada in November 1983 had seemed to increase the likelihood of military action against the Sandinista regime in Nicaragua. Although Álvarez supported a military solution to the "Nicaraguan problem," a significant faction of the Honduran officer corps held divergent convictions. These more nationalistic, more isolationist officers saw Álvarez as subservient to the United States, giving up more in terms of sovereignty than he received in aid. These officers also resented Álvarez's posturing in the media and his apparent aspirations to national leadership. On a more mundane level, certain officers also feared that Álvarez would force them out after he had solidified his power base within the officer corps. The prospect of early, involuntary retirement, with its attendant loss of licit and illicit income, prompted a clique of senior officers to move against Álvarez on March 31, 1984, seizing him and dispatching him on a flight to Miami.

The ouster of Álvarez produced a number of repercussions both in Honduran domestic politics and in Honduran-United States relations. The armed forces, which had appeared to be moving in a more activist and outward-looking direction under Álvarez, assumed a more isolationist stance toward regional relations and United States policy initiatives. Air Force Brigadier General Walter López Reyes, the new commander in chief, demanded further increases in military aid in return for Honduran cooperation in regional affairs. After some equivocation, López closed the CREM. He also scaled back Honduran-United States military exercises. On May 21, 1985, President Suazo Córdova and United States President Ronald W. Reagan signed a joint communiqué that amended a 1982 annex to the 1954 Military Assistance Agreement between the two countries. Although the new accord allowed the United States to expand and improve its temporary facilities at Palmerola Air Base near Comayagua, it generally limited Honduran cooperation in comparison to the terms of the 1982 annex.

By 1984 the armed forces under López began to exert pressure on the United States-backed Contra forces, the bulk of which operated from bases in the southern departments of El Paraíso and Olancho. Honduran foreign minister Edgardo Paz Barnica reflected the new attitude toward the Contras in January 1985, when he announced that the government planned to expel them from Honduras. Although that statement reflected bravado and frustration more than reality, the Honduran military took more active steps to pressure both the Contras and, indirectly, the United States government. In February 1985, the armed forces ordered the Contras to close a hospital that they had set up outside of Tegucigalpa. The Hondurans also ordered the Contras to shut down an office that had been used to receive official visitors, mainly from the United States. Around the same time, Honduran troops turned back two United States Department of State employees from a planned visit to a Contra training camp; the troops told the Americans that they lacked a newly required permit to enter the area.

The Nicaraguan Conflict

President Suazo Córdova had foreshadowed the Honduran ambivalence toward the Contras in a July 1983 letter to President Reagan, in which Suazo Córdova stated that "our people are beginning to ask with greater vigor if it is convenient to our own interests to be so intimately linked to the interests of the United States if we receive so little in exchange." Although 1983 and 1985 public opinion polls had shown that a majority of Hondurans supported United States policy in Central America, there was still a growing uneasiness over the country's role as reluctant host to Nicaraguan rebel forces. At the height of the conflict with the Sandinista Popular Army (Ejercito Popular Sandinista EPS), in the mid 1980s the Contra forces reportedly totaled between 12,000 and 17,000, depending on the source of the estimate. This force level rivaled that of the entire Honduran armed forces. This fact and the continued close ties between Honduras and the United States made it doubtful that the armed forces would expel the Nicaraguan rebels from Honduran territory by force. However, the prospect of an EPS victory over the Contras, which most observers considered inevitable, raised the disturbing prospect of a foreign armed force trapped on Honduran soil. Most Hondurans believed that, under such circumstances, the Nicaraguans would fail to assimilate well into the Honduran population and would resort to banditry in order to survive. Honduran politicians reflected little faith in the willingness of the United States to assist them should events take such a negative turn. Most believed that, following a Contra defeat, Washington would cut its losses and withdraw all support from the group.

Continued and sharply increased United States military aid to Honduras was the counterbalance to the prospect of United States withdrawal from the Nicaraguan conflict. For the years 1975-80, the total aid to Honduras had been US$16.3 million. From 1981-85, the total reached US$169 million. Meanwhile, the percentage of the military budget coming directly or indirectly from the United States increased from 7 percent in 1980 to 76 percent in 1985.

As the Nicaraguan conflict spread, Hondurans were left to ponder the merits of the deal the armed forces had brokered. On March 22, 1986, approximately 1,500 EPS ground troops crossed the Honduran border and engaged Contra forces near the hamlet of Las Vegas. The EPS withdrew into northern Nicaragua without making contact with Honduran forces. Honduran officials acknowledged the incursion publicly, but only after United States spokespersons had trumpeted the incident as proof of the Sandinistas' aggressive intentions toward their northern neighbor. Shortly thereafter, the United States Congress approved US$100 million in military aid to the Contra forces. Other EPS incursions into Honduran territory followed, notably in December 1986 and June 1987. How much human suffering passed in the frontier region without public notice by any government remained unknown. As in decades past, the spillover of the Nicaraguan conflict into more peaceful Honduras demonstrated the interrelatedness of events in all of the states of Central America.

The Struggle of Electoral Democracy: the Elections of 1985

The forced departure of Brigadier General Álvarez on March 31, 1984, and his succession by a group of officers who demonstrated less interest in political affairs than he had markedly changed the political situation prevailing in the country. President Suazo Córdova, previously restrained by his trepidations concerning lvarez, began to show signs of becoming a caudillo. Although the constitution forbade his reelection, Suazo Córdova conspired to nominate for the 1985 presidential elections Oscar Mejía Arellano, a fellow Rodista (the PLH faction founded by Modesto Rodas Alvarado). Every politician in Honduras recognized the octogenarian Mejía for what he was, namely someone who would perpetuate Suazo's control of the Presidential Palace. Nevertheless, Suazo

Córdova went about promoting Mejía's candidacy with every power at his disposal.

The potential key to a Mejía victory lay in the makeup of the Supreme Court of Justice, which could (under terms of the 1981 constitution) decide an election in which each candidate failed to receive a clear majority. As 1985 began, the Supreme Court contained a firm majority of Suazo Córdova supporters. The leadership of the Congress, both PLH and PNH, recognized the self-serving scenario that Suazo Córdova had set up. Moreover, they realized that the constitution granted power to the legislature to remove Supreme Court justices for cause. The Congress proceeded to do just that when fifty-three of its eighty-two deputies voted on March 29, 1985, to replace five of nine justices because of their alleged corruption. Five new justices quickly took the oath of office.

During the debate over the justices's corruption, Suazo Córdova had fulminated both publicly and privately, threatening to declare a state of emergency and close the Congress if the five lost their seats on the court. Although he stopped short of fulfilling that threat, troops did surround the Congress building temporarily after the deputies announced their action. Furthermore, military police took into custody Ramón Valladares Soto, the new president of the Supreme Court. Arrests of the four new other justices followed. A lower court judge charged the five with treason. On April 1, the judge filed treason charges against fifty-three legislative deputies who had voted to replace the five justices. The proceedings against the fifty-three, if pursued to its culmination, threatened to result in the revocation of legislators' legal immunity from prosecution.

The Congress rapidly reacted to Suazo's counterattack. On April 3, 1985, the assembly passed by a forty-nine to twenty-nine vote a motion censuring the president for his actions. In another action more calculated to curb the president's power, the legislature passed a bill establishing guidelines for primary elections within political parties. Had such guidelines been in place previously, the entire governmental crisis might have been avoided. Not surprisingly, Suazo Córdova vetoed the bill almost two weeks later, the day after the Rodista faction had endorsed his choice, Mejía, as the official presidential candidate of the PLH.

The resolution of the crisis demonstrated how little Honduras had progressed from the days when the military had guided events either directly or indirectly. During the early April days of the dispute between Suazo Córdova and the Congress, Brigadier General López had publicly declared himself and the armed forces neutral. As events began to degenerate, however, the officer corps moved to reconcile the antagonists. At first, the military sought to resolve the dispute through informal contacts. When that failed, the armed forces convened direct negotiations between presidential and legislative representatives, with military arbiters. By April 21, the talks produced an agreement. The leaders of Congress rescinded their dismissal of the five justices and dropped their demand for primary elections. Supreme Court President Valladares received his freedom. In a complicated arrangement, it was agreed that candidates of all political factions could run for president. The winner of the election would be the faction that received the most votes within the party (PLH, PNH, or other) that received the most total votes. The arrangement conveniently ignored the provision of the constitution stating that the president must be the candidate who receives a simple majority of the popular vote. Publicly, all parties expressed approval of the outcome. Although threatened union strike action had influenced the negotiations, the strongest factor in their outcome had been pressure from the armed forces leadership.

The unorthodox nature of the agreed-upon electoral procedures delayed adoption of new regulations until late in November. By that time, four PLH candidates, three PNH candidates, and several other minor party candidates had filed. The campaign appeared to pit two PLH candidates Mejía and San Pedro Sula engineer José Azcona Hoyo against the PNH's Rafael Leonardo Callejas Romero in a contest that saw the two PLH candidates criticize each other as much as, or more than, they did their opposition outside of their own party. The final vote count, announced on December 23, produced the result that the makeshift electoral regulations had made all but inevitable a president who garnered less than a majority of the total popular vote. The declared winner, Azcona, boasted less than 30 percent of the vote, as opposed to Callejas's 44 percent. But because the combined total of PLH candidates equaled 54 percent, Azcona claimed the presidential sash. Callejas lodged a protest, but it was short-lived and probably represented less than a sincere effort to challenge the agreement brokered by the military.

Azcona faced multiple national and regional problems as his inauguration took place on January 27, 1986. The new president's inaugural address noted the country's many social problems, but promised "no magic formulas" to solve them. He also noted the growing national debt and promised to adhere to foreign policies guided by the principle of nonintervention. Azcona's prospects for a successful presidency appeared dim, partly because his party's bloc in the Congress was still splintered, unlike the more united PNH deputies on the other side of the aisle. Beyond such parochial concerns, the crisis in Central America still raged on, presenting a daunting prospect for any Honduran leader.

From Contadora to Esquipulas

The Contadora Process

Although the crisis in Central America derived primarily from domestic pressures, the region's growing instability during the 1980s had drawn the attention and intervention of numerous foreign actors, chief among them the United States, the Soviet Union, and concerned nations of Latin America. The Contadora negotiating process (named for the Panamanian island where it was initiated in January 1983) sought to hammer out a solution among the five Central American nations through the mediation of the governments of Mexico, Venezuela, Colombia, and Panama. The negotiations proved arduous and protracted. By mid-1985, the talks had bogged down. The Nicaraguan delegates rejected discussion of democratization and internal reconciliation as an unwarranted intervention in their country's internal affairs. Honduras, El Salvador, Guatemala, and Costa Rica maintained that these provisions were necessary to ensure a lasting settlement.

Another major point of contention was the cessation of aid to insurgent groups, particularly United States aid to the Contras. Although the United States government was not a party to the Contadora negotiations, it was understood that the United States would sign a separate protocol agreeing to the terms of a final treaty in such areas as aid to insurgents, military aid and assistance to Central American governments, and joint military exercises in the region. The Nicaraguans demanded that any Contadora treaty call for an immediate end to Contra aid, whereas all the other Central American states and the mediating countries, with the exception of Mexico, downplayed the importance of such a provision. In addition, the Nicaraguan government raised objections to specific cuts in its military force levels, citing the imperatives of the counterinsurgency campaign and defense against a potential United States invasion. In an effort to break this impasse, the governments of Argentina, Brazil, Peru, and Uruguay announced in July 1985 that they would join the Contadora process as a "support group" in an effort to resolve the remaining points of contention and achieve a comprehensive agreement.

Despite the combined efforts of the original "core four" nations and the "support group," the Contadora process unofficially came to a halt during June 1986 when the Central American countries still failed to resolve their differences sufficiently to permit the signing of a final treaty draft. The United States Congress's approval of military aid to the Contras during the same month hampered the process, according to representatives of most of the mediating countries. Although the mediators vowed to continue their diplomatic efforts and did convene negotiating sessions subsequent to the unsuccessful June 6 meeting in Panama City, the Contadora process was clearly moribund.

After the Contadora process stalled, the regional consensus of opinion seemed to be that a streamlined, strictly Central American peace initiative stood a better chance of success than one that included countries outside the region. During the course of the Contadora negotiations, the Honduran government had sought to achieve an agreement that would settle the Nicaraguan conflict in such a way as to assure eventual reassimilation of the Contras into Nicaraguan society. At the same time, the Honduran military had sought to maintain its expanded relationship with the United States. Paradoxically, the Honduran government found itself espousing positions similar to those supported by its traditional adversary, El Salvador. As a new democracy, Honduras also enjoyed support from the government of Costa Rica, a more established democracy. The government of Guatemalan president Marco Vinicio Cerezo Arévalo established a more independent position, but still supported the concept of a diplomatic solution to Central America's troubles.

The Arias Plan

The five Central American presidents continued to seek a strictly Central American diplomatic solution. They held a meeting in May 1986 in Esquipulas, Guatemala, in an effort to work out their differences over the revised Contadora draft treaty. This meeting was a precursor of the process that in early 1987 superseded Contadora. The leading proponent and architect of this process was the president of Costa Rica, Oscar Arias Sánchez. After consultations with representatives of Honduras, El Salvador, Guatemala, and the United States, Arias announced on February 15, 1987, that he had presented a peace proposal to representatives of the other Central American states, with the exception of Nicaragua. The plan called for dialogue between governments and opposition groups, amnesty for political prisoners, cease-fires in ongoing insurgent conflicts, democratization, and free elections in all five regional states. The plan also called for renewed negotiations on arms reductions and an end to outside aid to insurgent forces.

Including the Nicaraguan administration in the negotiations was a sensitive issue. The first formal negotiating session to include representatives of that government took place in Tegucigalpa on July 31, 1987. That meeting of foreign ministers paved the way for an August 6, 1987, gathering of the five Central American presidents in Esquipulas. The negotiations, reportedly marked by blunt exchanges among the leaders, produced an agreement that many had considered unachievable only months before. The agreement, signed on August 7, called for the cessation of outside aid and support to insurgent forces but did allow the continuation of such aid to government forces. As a democratic government free from domestic insurgent problems, Honduras could easily comply with the terms of the Esquipulas accord.

The Central American Peace Agreement, variously referred to as "Esquipulas II" or the "Arias Plan," initially required the implementation of certain conditions by November 5, 1987. The conditions included establishing decrees of amnesty in those countries involved in insurgent conflicts, initiating dialogue between governments and unarmed political opposition groups or groups that had taken advantage of amnesty, undertaking efforts to negotiate cease-fires between governments and insurgent groups, ceasing to allow outside aid to insurgent forces, denying the use of each country's national territory to "groups trying to destabilize the governments of the countries of Central America," and ensuring conditions conducive to the development of a "pluralistic and participatory democratic process" in all of the signatory states.

Nicaragua's compliance with the Arias Plan was uneven by late 1988, and the process appeared to be losing momentum. The Nicaraguan government took a number of initial steps to comply with the treaty. These included allowing the independent daily *La Prensa* to reopen and the radio station of the Roman Catholic

Church to resume broadcasting, establishing a national reconciliation committee that incorporated representatives of the unarmed opposition, and eventually undertaking cease-fire negotiations with representatives of the Contras. The optimism engendered by the signing of a provisional cease-fire accord on March 23, 1988, at Sapoá, Nicaragua, however, had largely dissipated by July. During that month, the Nicaraguan government broke up a protest demonstration in the southern city of Nandaime, expelled the United States ambassador and seven other diplomats for alleged collaboration with the demonstrators, and again shut down *La Prensa* and the Roman Catholic radio station.

Accord in Nicaragua

Talks continued among the Central American presidents as they sought to resolve the insurgencies in El Salvador and Nicaragua. A series of summit meetings took place during 1989. The presidents agreed to a draft plan on February 14, 1989. The plan called for the demobilization and repatriation of Contra forces within ninety days, in return for elections. Nicaraguan president Daniel José Ortega Saavedra agreed to hold a February 1990 balloting. A foreign ministers' meeting also produced agreement on foreign (but non-United States) observers to supervise the demobilization.

The Central American leaders crafted the agreement largely without advice or guidance from the United States. Although the United States remained Honduras's leading supporter and ally, the United States administration gradually lost influence over events in Central America as the Esquipulas process played out. Having apparently neglected its relationship with President Azcona, the administration of George H.W. Bush (1989-93) turned to a more established connection, that between the United States government and the Honduran armed forces. Although Brigadier General López had been purged and exiled in February 1986, the armed forces maintained a pro-United States stance. After discussions with Bush administration envoys, the Honduran officer corps agreed that nonmilitary aid to the Contras should continue despite the February agreement. President Azcona, reportedly persuaded by the military, announced that humanitarian aid to the Contras would reduce the security threat to Honduras and would not violate the terms of the February 1989 agreement.

The ninety-day timetable established by the February 1989 agreement proved unworkable. In order to avoid losing momentum, the five presidents reconvened in Tela, Honduras, beginning on August 5, 1989. Once again, the presidents negotiated without input from the United States government. They produced a new schedule for Contra demobilization, with a deadline of December 5, 1989. The OAS agreed to supervise the process. Although the Bush administration expressed disapproval of the new agreement, the White House and United States Congress agreed that the Contras' aid would be cut off if the Nicaraguan rebels failed to disband; the United States Congress approved US$49.7 million in humanitarian aid to the Contras to be given through February 1990.

The December 5 deadline also proved overly optimistic. As the date approached, the Central American leaders again scheduled a summit. The first site selected was Managua. That venue changed to San José, Costa Rica, however, after the discovery of arms in the wreckage of a Nicaraguan aircraft that had crashed in El Salvador. The Salvadoran government subsequently suspended relations with Nicaragua, and an aura of conflict continued to hang over the summit. At one point, Azcona stormed out of a session after Nicaraguan president Ortega refused to drop Nicaragua's International Court of Justice suit against Honduras over the Contras' use of Honduran territory. The Nicaraguan government had previously agreed to drop the suit if the December 5 demobilization deadline were met. As the summit broke up without agreement, the Central American situation once again appeared dangerously unpredictable.

The unpredictability of events demonstrated itself once again in the Nicaraguan elections in February 1990. Contrary to most prognostications and opinion polls, opposition candidate Violeta Barrios de Chamorro handily defeated Ortega and the FSLN. Having been forced to hold free elections, the FSLN discovered that many Nicaraguans deeply resented the authoritarian rule of their revolutionary government. The Contra insurgency, which had plagued both Nicaragua and Honduras for years, slowly drew to a close.

Although Honduran president Azcona had began the process that eventually culminated in the resolution of the Nicaraguan conflict, another president would occupy the presidential palace as the Contras abandoned their camps in Honduras and marched south. The elections of November 26, 1989, were free of the makeshift electoral procedures that had rendered the 1985 balloting questionable. The PLH and PNH nominated one candidate each, rather than several. Carlos Flores Facusse, a Rodista and protégé of ex-president Suazo Córdova, won the PLH nomination and the right to oppose Rafael Leonardo Callejas, who had also carried the banner of the PNH when he lost in 1985. Callejas's convincing victory, by 50.2 to 44.5 percent, reflected public discontent with the PLH government's failure to translate increased foreign aid into improvements in the domestic economy. Callejas became the first opposition candidate to win an election in Honduras since 1932. All signs indicated that in the early 1990s, Honduras's democratic transition remained on course.

Geography

Honduras, situated at the widest point of Central America's isthmus, is the second biggest Central American nation. The triangular-shaped nation has an area of around 112,000 square kilometers. The Caribbean coast stretches 735 kilometers north from the mouth of the Rio Motagua on the west to the mouth of the Rio Coco on the east, at Cabo Gracias a Dios. The land boundary with Nicaragua runs along the 922-kilometer southeastern edge of the triangle, following the Rio Coco near the Caribbean Sea and then extending southwestward across rugged terrain to the Golfo de Fonseca on the Pacific Ocean. The triangle's southern tip is a 153-kilometer shoreline known as the Golfo de Fonseca, which opens into the Pacific Ocean. The 342-kilometer border with El Salvador and the 256-kilometer border with Guatemala form the western land boundary.

As part of its offshore territory, Honduras possesses a number of islands. In the Caribbean Sea, the islands of Roatán (Isla de Roatán), Utila, and Guanaja compose Islas de la Baha (Bay Islands), one of Honduras' eighteen departments. The biggest of the three islands, Roatán, is fifty kilometers long and five kilometers broad. The Islas de la Bahia archipelago also includes a number of smaller islands, including the islets of Barbareta (Isla Barbareta), Santa Elena (Isla Santa Elena), and Morat (Isla Morat) (Isla Morat). The Islas Santanillas, historically known as the Swan Islands, are located farther out in the Caribbean. A variety of tiny islands and keys, including Cayos Zapotillos and Cayos Cochinos, are close. The principal islands under Honduran jurisdiction in the Golfo de Fonseca are El Tigre, Zacate Grande (Isla Zacate Grande), and Exposición (Isla Exposición).

Boundary Disputes

A two-centuries-old border dispute between El Salvador and Honduras appears to have been resolved in 1993. At issue in this territorial dispute was ownership of six contested *bolsones* (pockets) of land encompassing a total area of 436.9 square kilometers as well as two islands (Meanguera and El Tigre) in the Golfo de Fonseca, and right of passage for Honduras to the Pacific Ocean from its southern coast.

The origins of the boundary dispute date back to the eighteenth century when colonial boundaries were ill defined. In the late nineteenth century, numerous attempts at mediation failed to settle the dispute. The issue continued to fester in the twentieth century and was a contributing factor in the outbreak of war between the two countries in 1969. The General Peace Treaty, signed by El Salvador and Honduras on October 30, 1980, in Lima, Peru, represented the first real breakthrough on this border dispute. The peace treaty stated that the two parties agreed to submit the boundary dispute to the International Court of Justice (ICJ) in The Hague if they failed to reach a border agreement after five years of negotiations. By 1985 the two countries had not reached an agreement. In 1986 the case reached the ICJ, which handed down a ruling on September 11, 1992. Both countries accepted the ICJ decision, and a commission was established to decide the citizenship of residents of the *bolsones*.

Of the 436.9 square kilometers in dispute, 300.6 square kilometers were granted to Honduras, and 136.3 were granted to El Salvador. Of the six *bolsones*, Honduras was awarded complete control of one and approximately 80 percent of another. The remaining four were split with El Salvador. El Salvador was awarded possession of the island of Meanguera, and Honduras was awarded control of the island of El Tigre. More importantly for Honduras, the ICJ ruling assured Honduras's free passage to the Pacific Ocean. The ICJ also decided that the Golfo de Fonseca does not represent international waters because of the two countries' shared history as provinces of the same colonial power and subsequent membership in the United Provinces of Central America. The court ruled, rather, that the Golfo de Fonseca is a condominium, with control being shared by El Salvador, Honduras, and Nicaragua. The latter country also has a coastline on the gulf. The decision allowed for the possibility that the three nations could divide the waters at a later date if they wished to do so.

Topography

Honduras has three distinct topographical regions: an extensive interior highland area and two narrow coastal lowlands. The interior, which constitutes approximately 80 percent of the country's terrain, is mountainous. The larger Caribbean lowlands in the north and the Pacific lowlands bordering the Golfo de Fonseca are characterized by alluvial plains.

Interior Highlands

The interior highlands are the most prominent feature of Honduran topography. Composing approximately 80 percent of the country's total area, these mountain areas are home to the majority of the population. Because the rugged terrain has made the land difficult to traverse and equally difficult to cultivate, this area has not been highly developed. The soil here is poor; Honduras lacks the rich volcanic ash found in other Central American countries. Until the early part of the twentieth century, the highlands economy consisted primarily of mining and livestock.

In the west, Honduras's mountains blend into the mountain ranges of Guatemala. The western mountains have the highest peaks, with the Pico Congolón at an elevation of 2,500 meters and the Cerro de Las Minas at 2,850 meters. These mountains are woodland covered with mainly pine forests.

In the east, the mountains merge with those in Nicaragua. Although generally not as high as the mountains near the

Guatemalan border, the eastern ranges possess some high peaks, such as the Montaña de la Flor at 2,300 meters, El Boquerón (Monte El Boquerón) at 2,485 meters, and Pico Bonito at 2,435 meters.

One of the most prominent features of the interior highlands is a depression that runs from the Caribbean Sea to the Golfo de Fonseca. This depression splits the country's cordilleras into eastern and western parts and provides a relatively easy transportation route across the isthmus. Widest at its northern end near San Pedro Sula, the depression narrows as it follows the upper course of the Río Humuya. Passing first through Comayagua and then through narrow passes south of the city, the depression widens again as it runs along the border of El Salvador into the Golfo de Fonseca.

Scattered throughout the interior highlands are numerous flatfloored valleys, 300 to 900 meters in elevation, which vary in size. The floors of the large valleys provide sufficient grass, shrubs, and dry woodland to support livestock and, in some cases, commercial agriculture. Subsistence agriculture has been relegated to the slopes of the valleys, with the limitations of small-sized holdings, primitive technology, and low productivity that traditionally accompany hillside cultivation. Villages and towns, including the capital, Tegucigalpa, are tucked in the larger valleys.

Vegetation in the interior highlands is varied. Much of the western, southern, and central mountains are open woodland supporting pine forest interspersed with some oak, scrub, and grassy clearings. The ranges toward the east are primarily continuous areas of dense, broad-leaf evergreen forest. Around the highest peaks, remnants of dense rain forest that formerly covered much of the area are still found.

The Caribbean Lowlands

This area of river valleys and coastal plains, which most Honduras call "the north coast," or simply "the coast," has traditionally been Honduras's most exploited region. The central part of the Caribbean lowlands, east of La Ceiba, is a narrow coastal plain only a few kilometers wide. To the east and west of this section, however, the Caribbean lowlands widen and in places extend inland a considerable distance along broad river valleys. The broadest river valley, along the Río Ulúa near the Guatemalan border, is Honduras's most developed area. Both Puerto Cortés, the country's largest port, and San Pedro Sula, Honduras's industrial capital, are located here.

To the east, near the Nicaraguan border, the Caribbean lowlands broaden to an extensive area known as the Mosquitia. Unlike the western part of the Caribbean lowlands, the Mosquitia is Honduras's least-developed area. Underpopulated and culturally distinct from the rest of the country, the area consists of inland savannah with swamps and mangrove near the coast. During times of heavy rainfall, much of the savannah area is covered by shallow water, making transportation by means other than a shallow-draft boat almost impossible

Pacific Lowlands

The smallest physiographic region of Honduras, the Pacific lowlands, is a strip of land averaging twenty-five kilometers wide on the north shore of the Golfo de Fonseca. The land is flat, becoming swampy near the shores of the gulf, and is composed mostly of alluvial soils washed down from the mountains. The gulf is shallow and the water rich in fish and mollusks. Mangroves along the shore make shrimp and shellfish particularly abundant by providing safe and abundant breeding areas amid their extensive networks of underwater roots.

Several islands in the gulf fall under Honduras's jurisdiction. The two largest, Zacate Grande and El Tigre, are eroded volcanoes, part of the chain of volcanoes that extends along the Pacific coast of

Central America. Both islands have volcanic cones more than 700 meters in elevation that serve as markers for vessels entering Honduras's Pacific ports.

Climate

Although all of Honduras lies within the tropics, the climatic types of each of the three physiographic regions differ. The Caribbean lowlands have a tropical wet climate with consistently high temperatures and humidity, and rainfall fairly evenly distributed throughout the year. The Pacific lowlands have a tropical wet and dry climate with high temperatures but a distinct dry season from November through April. The interior highlands also have a distinct dry season, but, as is characteristic of a tropical highland climate, temperatures in this region decrease as elevation increases.

Unlike in more northerly latitudes, temperatures in the tropics vary primarily with elevation instead of with the season. Land below 1,000 meters is commonly known as *tierra caliente* (hot land), between 1,000 and 2,000 meters *tierra templada* (temperate land), and above 2,000 meters *tierra fría* (cold land). Both the Caribbean and Pacific lowlands are *tierra caliente*, with daytime highs averaging between 28° C and 32° C throughout the year. In the Pacific lowlands, April, the last month of the dry season, brings the warmest temperatures; the rainy season is slightly cooler, although higher humidity during the rainy season makes these months feel more uncomfortable. In the Caribbean lowlands, the only relief from the year-round heat and humidity comes during December or January when an occasional strong cold front from the north (a *norte*) brings several days of strong northwest winds and slightly cooler temperatures.

The interior highlands range from *tierra templada* to *tierra fría*. Tegucigalpa, in a sheltered valley and at an elevation of 1,000 meters, has a pleasant climate, with an average high temperature ranging from 30° C in April, the warmest month, to 25° C in January, the coolest. Above 2,000 meters, temperatures can fall to near freezing at night, and frost sometimes occurs.

Rain falls year round in the Caribbean lowlands but is seasonal throughout the rest of the country. Amounts are copious along the north coast, especially in the Mosquitia, where the average rainfall is 2,400 millimeters. Nearer San Pedro Sula, amounts are slightly less from November to April, but each month still has considerable precipitation. The interior highlands and Pacific lowlands have a dry season, known locally as "summer," from November to April. Almost all the rain in these regions falls during the "winter," from May to September. Total yearly amounts depend on surrounding topography; Tegucigalpa, in a sheltered valley, averages only 1,000 millimeters of precipitation.

Honduras lies within the hurricane belt, and the Caribbean coast is particularly vulnerable to hurricanes or tropical storms that travel inland from the Caribbean. Hurricane Francelia in 1969 and Tropical Storm Alleta in 1982 affected thousands of people and caused extensive damage to crops. Hurricane Fifi in 1974 was the worst natural disaster in recent Honduran history; more than 8,000 people were killed, and nearly the entire banana crop was destroyed. Hurricanes occasionally form over the Pacific and move north to affect southern Honduras, but Pacific storms are generally less severe and their landfall rarer.

Rivers

Honduras is a water-rich country. The most important river in Honduras is the Ulúa, which flows 400 kilometers to the Caribbean through the economically important Valle de Sula. Numerous other rivers drain the interior highlands and empty north into the Caribbean. These other rivers are important, not as transportation routes, but because of the broad fertile valleys they have produced.

Rivers also define about half of Honduras's international borders. The Río Goascorán, flowing to the Golfo de Fonseca, and the Río Lempa define part of the border between El Salvador and Honduras. The Río Coco marks about half of the border between Nicaragua and Honduras.

Despite an abundance of rivers, large bodies of water are rare. Lago de Yojoa, located in the west-central part of the country, is the sole natural lake in Honduras. This lake is twenty-two kilometers long and at its widest point measures fourteen kilometers. Several large, brackish lagoons open onto the Caribbean in northeast Honduras. These shallow bodies of water allow limited transportation to points along the coast.

The Society

The majority of Honduran society is rural and impoverished. The country's general level of life is among the lowest in the Western Hemisphere. Foreign and internal evaluations of the country have concentrated on poverty to the extent that this assessment dominates the Honduran people's viewpoint.

Almost all social indicators show Honduras trailing behind in terms of growth. Annual per capita income is poor, health services are severely lacking, newborn and child death rates are high, and literacy and other educational indicators are low. In 1993, the majority of Honduras' population remained impoverished, and a rapid pace of population growth rendered alleviation of poverty in the near future impossible.

The fact that Honduras has a low population density seems to be a plus. However, an abundance of land has not secured the availability of cultivable land. The geography is mostly mountainous, with just a few tiny coastal flats. Many fertile lands are utilised for export crops and are not accessible to small farmers. Agribusinesses based on bananas (and some pineapple) thrive on the country's most fertile territory, the Caribbean coastal lowlands. Since the 1950s, area usable for agriculture has actually declined as cropland has been turned to rangeland to serve a burgeoning cattle export sector.

Honduran society had a crisis of trust in the 1980s as a result of the country's persistent underdevelopment. Indeed, economic and social forces created an intense feeling of disorientation in Honduran society throughout that decade. The combination of a global economic crisis, a rapid increase in crime, and the lack of an independent police force and court system left the ordinary person feeling vulnerable.

Despite the sad statistics, Honduran society has various assets. Positive elements include a relatively large number of grassroots groups, a peasant movement that has persisted even during times of persecution, and a corporatist political system in which organizations and classes make political demands rather than political parties. The lack of civil conflict and the high degree of terrorism witnessed by neighboring nations are also positives.

The dilemma for Honduras in the future is how to cope with extreme poverty while avoiding the repression and violence that poverty typically brings.

Population

In 1993 Honduras still had a low population density despite explosive population growth during the second half of the twentieth century and significant immigration from neighboring countries. The population was also slightly more than 50 percent rural and unevenly distributed in the mountainous areas around the capital and near the Salvadoran border, and in the Río Ulúa valley. Rapid internal migration, however, was expected to change Honduras from a rural highlands nation in the twentieth century to an urban one with large segments living in coastal lowlands in the twenty-first century.

Population Density

Although Honduras, with forty-six inhabitants per square kilometer, has a relatively low population density, especially when compared to its neighbors to the west, uneven distribution has contributed to overpopulation in certain areas. The five mountainous departments bordering El Salvador (Ocotepeque, Lempira, Intibucá, La Paz, and Valle) have a much higher population density than the four sparsely populated departments in the east (Colón, Olancho, Gracias a Dios, and El Paraíso). The country's second-largest and least-populated department, Gracias a Dios, had a population density of only 2.5 inhabitants per square kilometer in 1989. Honduras's only densely populated lowland area is the Río Ulúa valley. In 1989 the department of Cortés, on the west bank of the Río Ulúa, had a population density of 188 inhabitants per square kilometer.

Honduras is the only country in Central America with an urban population distributed between two large centers. Whereas other Central American capitals are home to more than 50 percent of their countries' urban populations, Tegucigalpa's percentage of total urban population is considerably lower. The difference is accounted for by the growth of San Pedro Sula. By the beginning of the twenty-first century, Tegucigalpa and San Pedro Sula are projected to account for nearly 73 percent of the population living in urban areas. The two cities are also projected to account for 25 percent of the total population of Honduras by the end of the twentieth century.

Rural-to-Urban Migration

The vast majority of the rural-to-urban population shift has been the result of migration from the southwestern departments (Ocotepeque, Lempira, Intibucá, La Paz, and Valle) to cities in the departments on or near the Caribbean coast (Cortés, Yoro, Atlántida, and Colón) and to Tegucigalpa (in Francisco Morazán department in the central highlands). During the earlier part of the twentieth century, employment opportunities in the newly established banana plantations attracted many people from southern and western Honduras to the Caribbean coast. Cities on the banks of the Río Ulúa, especially El Progreso, experienced impressive growth as a result of this migration from the south. Migration from the mountainous southwest sparked tremendous development in the city of San Pedro Sula. The search for employment also led many to Tegucigalpa, even though the capital has never been a center for industry or agriculture.

Demographers have predicted that, unless significant social and economic reforms are instituted, the rural-to-urban migration trend so prevalent in the twentieth century not only will continue but also will probably increase. Although Honduras is still primarily an agrarian society, urban centers have grown considerably since the 1920s. Analysts speculate that urban centers will continue to expand as a result of internal migration and national population growth.

In the second half of the twentieth century, Tegucigalpa in particular experienced sharp increases in its population. During the 1950s, Tegucigalpa's population increased nearly 75 percent. The following decade brought a population rate increase of more than 80 percent. In 1980 Tegucigalpa had a population of 400,000. By 1989 the population had soared to 576,661. This increase in population has practically crippled the already fragile infrastructure of the city. Housing is woefully inadequate, and a large percentage of the residents either lack running water altogether or receive inadequate amounts.

During the period between 1950 and 1980, San Pedro Sula had a population growth rate that exceeded that of Tegucigalpa. In the 1980s, the annual growth rate dropped somewhat and was less than that of Tegucigalpa (3.7 percent and 4.4 percent, respectively). In 1988 the population of San Pedro Sula stood at 287,350. Whereas San Pedro Sula has dealt more successfully with its population growth, it is nonetheless challenged to meet the housing, services, and employment needs of new inhabitants.

Other urban centers experiencing a high population growth rate are La Ceiba, on the Caribbean, and El Progreso, in the agricultural valley of the Río Ulúa. La Ceiba is the third-largest city in Honduras. In 1988 it had a population of 68,764 and an annual population growth rate of 3.2 percent. El Progreso is the country's fourth-largest city. The 1988 population of this city was 60,058 and the annual growth rate 4.5 percent. The populations of both La Ceiba and El Progreso are expected to exceed 100,000 by the year 2000.

The majority of migrants in Honduras are very young, ranging from their teens to their early twenties. Most male migrants gravitate toward developing agricultural areas, especially the Caribbean coast. Because women traditionally have a more limited choice of employment, their occupational skills are similarly limited. Among the many incentives for their migration are escape from economic hardship, as well as escape from marriage and childbearing at a very young age. The majority of women migrants seek domestic employment or work as street vendors in urban areas. In the early 1990s, an increasing number of women have been seeking employment in the *maquiladoras*, or assembly factories. Many others become prostitutes. Male urban migrants seek jobs in artisan shops, with merchants, and as laborers. Employment opportunities for the new migrants remain spotty, however, as the industrial and commercial sectors in Honduras have not created enough jobs to absorb the population coming from the rural areas.

Regional Emigration

Since the early twentieth century, Honduras has had the challenge of absorbing thousands of immigrants from neighboring countries. Political tensions throughout Central America have been a key factor behind much of the immigration. The number of immigrants from El Salvador looking for land or jobs was especially high between the early twentieth century and the onset of the 1969 Soccer War between El Salvador and Honduras. A significant number of Salvadoran immigrants worked in the banana plantations during the 1930s and 1940s.

Armed conflict in Nicaragua, Guatemala, and El Salvador in the 1980s resulted in the arrival of more than 60,000 refugees. Most of these refugees live near their respective borders, and the majority are women and children. Throughout the 1980s, Nicaraguan refugees continued to arrive in Honduras as the war between Nicaragua's Sandinista government and the Nicaraguan Resistance forces (known as the Contras, short for *contrarevolucionarios* counterrevolutionaries in Spanish) intensified. By the early 1990s, Honduras hosted an estimated 250,000 refugees or immigrants from Central America.

Population Growth

In the second half of the twentieth century, Honduras underwent explosive population growth. In the 1910 census, the annual rate of population growth barely exceeded 1.5 percent. By 1950 it had reached 3 percent. From 1960 to 1990, the population growth rate climbed to 3.3 percent. By 1992 the annual population growth had slowed somewhat, but only to an estimated 2.8 percent.

The country's high birth rate has led Honduras's population to double about every twenty-five years. The 1950 census counted 1,368,605 inhabitants, almost twice as many as the 1926 census recorded. By 1974 the population had almost doubled once again. As of July 1992, the population was estimated to be 5,092,776.

Several factors have contributed to the rapid population rise. Honduras has consistently maintained high birth rates during the twentieth century. The crude birth rate (CBR the annual number of births per 1,000 inhabitants) from the beginning to the midpoint of the century fluctuated between 41.7 and 44.5 births per 1,000 inhabitants. From around 1950 to 1975, Honduras had the highest CBR in Latin America. Since the mid-1970s, the CBR has dropped and steadied somewhat. In 1990 the CBR stood at 39 births per 1,000 inhabitants.

The total fertility rate (TFR-the average number of children a woman would bear in her lifetime) had dropped to 7.5 children per woman by the early 1970s. Since the 1970s, the TFR in Honduras has declined. In 1990 it was 5.2, and the projected TFR for the year 2000 is 4.1.

In 1993, however, the TFR varied considerably according to a woman's residence in rural or urban areas and according to income levels. Rural women had an average of 8.7 children while urban women had 5.3 children. The TFR for all upper and middle income women (rural and urban) was 5.8, while among lower income women it was approximately 8.0.

Regional differences in birth rates, coupled with internal migration, are expected to change Honduras's population distribution. The department of Cortés, with a high population growth rate, and the departments of Colón and Gracias a Dios, heretofore thinly populated areas in the northeast, are expected to become the country's fastest growing areas. The emerging population pattern is one of significant growth in the central highlands near Tegucigalpa and along the entire Caribbean coast region from San Pedro Sula east to Gracias a Dios. The departments bordering El Salvador, in the southwest region of the country, are expected to have the slowest population growth rate.

The absorption of this expanding population represents a serious challenge to the Honduran government. Already inadequate health services, as well as poor educational, employment, and housing opportunities, will be increasingly burdened by a rapidly growing and young population. In 1989 slightly more than 2 million Hondurans, or 45 percent, were between one and fourteen years old. Frustrated expectations for a better standard of living among this youthful population raise the possibility of unrest in the future.

Social Sectors

Honduran society, for the most part, mirrors other Latin American countries in terms of its social classes and sectors. Distribution of wealth is uneven, with a small minority of the population (increasingly made up of members of the military) controlling national politics and wealth. Capital is largely obtained through ownership of large landed estates, collaboration with foreign entrepreneurial enterprises, and privileges granted to the military.

In sharp contrast to the small wealthy class, the vast majority of the population is made up of subsistence farmers and agricultural laborers who live in increasing poverty. Since the 1950s, a small middle class has emerged from the ranks of the poor and the artisan sectors. This new middle class had become moderately well off by the 1990s. However, the middle class and especially the poor were extremely hard hit during the economic crisis of the 1980s. Both classes saw many of the modest economic gains they had made in the previous three decades wiped out.

Background

Although the class structure in Honduras is similar to that in other Latin American countries, the manner in which these classes interact presents less conflict than is exhibited by Honduras's immediate neighbors. The relative lack of tension in class relations raises the possibility that Honduras might avoid the social and political violence that has plagued Guatemala, El Salvador, and Nicaragua. Political dynamics peculiar to Honduras tend to lessen social pressures, although it is still possible that class tensions, growing poverty among the majority of the population, and increased concentration of wealth in a minority could result in violence in the future.

The low level of social tension in Honduras has its origins in the country's colonial and early republican history. During the colonial period, the province that later became Honduras was a backwater in the territories held by Spain. Because much of the indigenous population either had been exterminated or had died of disease, the province was sparsely populated. Ethnically, this meant that Honduras had a more homogeneous mestizo culture than most other Spanish colonies. The area was isolated because the majority of Honduras's population settled in the central and western highlands, far from the main transportation route that linked the southern and northern regions of the Spanish Empire. Furthermore, the area lacked any significant mineral deposits or other easily exploitable wealth. Consequently, the colonial elite in Honduras came to be defined by their control of the province's political system rather than by their accumulation of wealth. In later centuries, the absence of coffee exporting concerns in Honduras became another factor differentiating it from its neighbors. In most of Central America, large coffee plantations resulted in a wealthy elite. The accumulation of large fortunes by a land-owning minority took place much later in Honduras during the twentieth century, when much of the wealth from the new banana businesses went to foreign investors who owned the banana companies.

Advocates for Social Change

During the twentieth century, the corporatist system of politics that has emerged has eased the intensity of the demands placed on the state by the rural and urban poor. The relative openness of Honduran politics and the degree of legitimacy given to working class demands have resulted in a system in which the organizations representing lower sectors of society can be highly organized and even militant without calling for the overthrow of the system itself. This militancy has made organized labor a political force since the 1950s and has resulted in many labor reforms. Peasant militancy, for example, has made possible the agrarian reform movement. According to some analysts, Honduras has achieved a level of political organization on the part of labor unions and peasant organizations that remains unparalleled in most of Central America. Reform has been uneven, however, and political and social reform movements stagnated in the 1970s and 1980s. In the early 1990s, the central problems of poverty and underdevelopment remained pervasive.

The military's participation in Honduran politics has been, in one sense, the action of another interest group. The military in Honduras has not emerged as an organization for the sons of the elite, as has been the case in most of Latin America, but rather as an organization that cuts across economic and class lines. This fact has meant a greater divergence of purpose and interests between the traditional Honduran elite and the armed forces. The decision-making structure within the military also allows for a degree of dissent within the organization, resulting in less resistance to social reforms.

The relatively open political discourse found in Honduras is aided by the ability of other social institutions to take advantage of the country's freedom of expression. Although in general the Honduran press tends toward conservative positions, it is free of direct government control. Control of the press is exercised more through cooptation than by censorship. Several independent radio stations are powerful forces in Honduras, a country that has a high illiteracy rate. The independent position of the National Autonomous University of Honduras (Universidad Nacional Autónoma de Honduras UNAH), which as a rule holds liberal positions, also contributes to the variety of opinions that can be heard.

The Honduran Roman Catholic Church also has been a force pressing for social change and reform, although its role has varied and, in many instances, has been contradictory throughout the years. The role of the church as advocate for change gained ground in the late 1960s after Vatican Council II. The church's role gathered momentum after the meeting of the Latin American Conference of Bishops in Medellín, Colombia in 1968. The Roman Catholic Church in Honduras came to hold the view that its members should become active agents of social change. In Honduras, foreign clergy in particular played a major role in social activism. By the 1970s, the Roman Catholic Church in Honduras had come to be perceived as radical, and in 1971 various Roman Catholic Church organizations joined with those of the Christian Democratic Movement of

Honduras (Movimiento Demócrata Cristiano de Honduras MDCH) to form the Coordinating Council for Development (Consejo Coordinador de Desarrollo Concorde). The impact of this activism was felt down to the parish level.

Differences of opinion emerged within the Roman Catholic Church in the late 1970s, however, regarding its approach to social change. Certain orders of clergy, particularly the Jesuits (Society of Jesus) and various priests, advocated even greater activism than the church hierarchy supported. The hierarchy's opposition to further change was evident when it withdrew Roman Catholic organizations from the Concorde. As Central America took central stage in the Cold War in the 1970s and 1980s because of events in Nicaragua and El Salvador, activist priests were accused of being communists. Tensions between the church's hierarchy and activist priests eased in the 1990s, however, with the decline of insurgency in the area.

Increased political conservatism and repression during the 1980s resulted in the emergence of a great number of grass-roots organizations. Along with labor unions and peasant organizations, the emerging groups advocated vigilance concerning human rights and exerted pressure on the authorities to reveal the whereabouts of disappeared citizens.

These new grass-roots groups, as well as the press, the UNAH, and the Roman Catholic Church, all contributed to the preservation of a political system with relative freedom of expression. The attempts at reform initiated by these groups, however, have not met with complete success. Although the government and military have at times opted for compromise in the face of reform demands, the organizations have also had to endure periods of threatened and real repression.

The Upper Class

Although the upper class has enjoyed privileges and wealth far greater than the general population, the Honduran elite has been both economically and politically the weakest oligarchy in Central America. This relative lack of power is partly the result of the dominant role of foreign investment in Honduras since the early twentieth century. Until about 1900, the Honduran elite was involved in rural landholding in the interior highlands and valleys. To this day, some hacendados (large hacienda owners) continue to live on their rural estates. Until the arrival of the banana companies, Hondurans had avoided the underpopulated, inhospitable Caribbean lowlands infamous for their heat and pestilence. Even after banana plantations were established in the Caribbean lowlands at the turn of the century, the interior highlands elite largely maintained its status quo.

With the development of cotton and livestock export businesses following World War II, the traditional Honduran elite became more economically active. In response to the beef markets that opened after the war, commercial production of cattle also became quite profitable. Between 1950 and 1980, cattle production more than tripled in Honduras. This period witnessed a marked acceleration in the concentration of land holdings and wealth. These changes took place mostly at the expense of lands formerly used for food production. As land title disputes and seizures proliferated, social tensions in rural Honduras increased drastically.

With wealth its only defining criterion, the upper class in Honduras is not particularly cohesive and has often split into divergent groups over political and economic issues. Competing business associations have served as vehicles for the disputing factions. Certain factions of the elite are more conservative, whereas others advocate a more liberal and open path to economic development. As a result of their differences, members of the upper class are willing to participate in an open dialogue and form alliances with other sectors and classes. In the 1950s, business interests supported striking workers in foreign-owned corporations.

At times, factions of the elite have supported social change while their conservative counterparts have fiercely opposed it. In the 1970s, the military, labor, and peasant organizations joined forces with the more progressive faction of the elite to support a military regime with a reform platform. Probably because all sectors keep a stake in the system, Honduras has avoided fundamental challenges to its social structure and overthrow of its political system.

The twentieth century has seen the military become a part of Honduras's elite. In the mid-1950s, the armed forces in Honduras underwent a transformation. With aid and training primarily from the United States, the military went from being what was, in effect, an array of provincial militias to a modern national institution. Because the military in Honduras had never been an institution favored by the traditional elite, the military has emerged as an independent member of the upper sector of society.

The Middle Class

In 1993 the middle class in Honduras is still a small, albeit growing, sector. Inclusion in this sector is best defined by economic factors and by occupation. Except for merchants, an equally important factor in classifying a person as middle class appears to be completion of a higher education. Included among middle class ranks are professionals, students, farmers, merchants, business employees, and civil servants. Although a well-paying occupation is crucial for movement up to the middle sector, incomes for this group are still relatively low.

One factor limiting the size of the middle class is the slow growth of industry and commerce in Honduras. Employment opportunities are scarce. The growth of the middle class in the Caribbean coast region has been directly tied to that area's industries and foreign enterprises. The success of merchants in the north has resulted from the markets created by workers employed in the area's agribusinesses. The middle class in Honduras has not been politically active as a unified group, although many in its ranks are politically active through unions, church groups, or other organizations.

The Lower Class

Traditionally, the poor in Honduras have lived predominantly in rural areas. The lack of economic opportunity in rural areas and the subsequent migration to the cities have led to an increasing number of urban poor.

During the colonial period, the low population density in the country made land readily available for small subsistence farmers. When the concentration of land for cotton and cattle export began in the 1950s, the situation in the rural areas changed. By the 1960s, poor rural families were struggling for survival on smaller parcels of land that had ever-decreasing rates of fertility and productivity. By 1965 landlessness had become a problem.

The increase in the number of landless peasants led to even greater numbers migrating to cities in search of employment and in the emergence of a peasant movement in national politics. The majority of those unable to practice subsistence farming remained in rural areas, however, and sought work as farm workers; 62 percent of the labor force in 1993 was in agriculture. Other displaced peasants migrated to the cities in search of employment in the service sector (20 percent of the total labor force in 1993), manufacturing (9 percent of the total labor force), and construction (3 percent of the total labor force). Still others joined the peasant movement and migrated to areas where cooperative enterprises were being established or to areas where members of militant peasant groups were appropriating land.

The poorest peasants still practice subsistence farming in plots of five hectares or less. Many others work as sharecroppers or rent land for cash. The majority of peasants are forced to seek work as full-time or part-time laborers, depending on the season and the size of the farms on which they are employed. At best, this work provides income to supplement the meager earnings from their own small parcels of land. At worst, this work represents their sole source of income.

Although official unemployment figures are not very high, underemployment is widespread in the countryside and is increasingly a problem in urban centers as well. Underemployment (ranging between 15 and 75 percent) is usually a result of the seasonal nature of most of the available agricultural work. During the 1980s, the level of underemployment also rose in areas of the Caribbean coast where banana and sugarcane plantations are located. Although work in sugarcane fields is seasonal, banana plantations are a source of long-term contracts or even permanent employment. The labor surplus in the interior highlands is evidence of the severe economic plight of most Hondurans.

In the 1980s, land pressures, an increasing number of landless peasants, and the declining standard of living of the peasantry and working class galvanized the ranks of peasant organizations and labor unions. The first national peasant group to organize, in the 1950s, was the National Federation of Honduran Peasants (Federación Nacional de Campesinos de Honduras Fenach). The National Association of Honduran Peasants (Asociación Nacional de Campesinos de Honduras Anach) was established in 1962 as a competing association. By the time of the economic crisis of the 1980s, both associations had become equally militant and confrontational. The National Union of Peasants (Unión Nacional de Campesinos UNC) was formed in the 1960s. It began as a militant organization with roots in the international Christian socialist movement, but by 1993 it was a less combative association. Many other politically active peasant organizations operated in Honduras. Their roles and strategies have varied from alienating the government and military with land takeovers and other militant tactics to a joint agricultural project with the military in 1989.

Since the 1954 banana workers' strike, the labor movement in Honduras has been the strongest in Central America; in 1992, 40 percent of urban labor and 20 percent of rural labor were unionized. Unions are strongest in the public sector, the agricultural sector, and the manufacturing sector. Strategies used by the labor movement range from providing crucial support to sympathetic administrations to adopting more combative positions during general strikes.

Although the labor and peasant movements represent interest groups that cannot be politically ignored, their influence has varied considerably since the 1950s. The two movements were weakened somewhat by repeated government attempts to divide the organizations. They were also weakened by internal divisions and the presence of opportunistic individuals in leadership positions. The economic crisis of the 1980s and the imposition of the economic adjustment policies during that decade have also taken a toll on these organizations. Confrontations between these groups and the government were frequent in the early 1990s. On more than one occasion, strikes in key sectors of the economy led to the government's calling in the army.

Family

The family is the fundamental social unit in Honduras, providing a bulwark in the midst of political upheavals and economic reversals. People emphasize the trust, the assistance, and the solidarity that kin owe to one another. Family loyalty is an ingrained and unquestioned virtue; from early childhood, individuals learn that relatives are to be trusted and relied on, whereas those outside the family are, implicitly at least, suspect. In all areas of life and at every level of society, a person looks to family and kin for both social identity and assistance.

In general, the extent to which families interact, and the people with whom they interact, depends on their degree of prosperity. Families with relatively equal resources share and cooperate. Where there is marked disparity in the wealth of various branches of a family, the more prosperous branches try to limit the demands made by the poorer ones. On the one hand, generosity is held in high esteem, and failure to care for kin in need is disparaged; but, on the other hand, families prefer to help their immediate relatives and to bestow favors on those who are able to reciprocate. A needy relative might receive the loan of a piece of land, some wage labor, or occasional gifts of food. Another type of assistance is a form of adoption by which poorer families give a child to more affluent relatives to raise. The adopting family is expected to care for the child and to see that he or she receives a proper upbringing. The children, however, are frequently little better than unpaid domestic help. Implicit in the arrangement is the understanding that the child's biological family, too, will receive assistance from the adopting family.

Kinship serves as metaphor for relations of trust in general. Where a kin tie is lacking, or where individuals wish to reinforce one, a relationship of *compadrazgo* is often established. Those so linked are *compadres* (co-parents or godparents). In common with much of Latin America, strong emotional bonds link *compadres*. *Compadres* use the formal *usted* instead of *tú* in addressing one another, even if they are kin. Sexual relations between *compadres* are regarded as incestuous. *Compadres* are commonly chosen at baptism and marriage, but the relationship extends to the two sets of parents. The tie between the two sets of parents is expected to be strong and enduring. Any breach of trust merits the strongest community censure.

There are three accepted forms of marriage: civil, religious, and free unions. Both serial monogamy and polygamous unions are socially accepted. Annulment is difficult to obtain through the Roman Catholic Church; this fact, in addition to the expense involved, makes couples reluctant to undertake a religious marriage. Civil marriage is relatively common. Divorce in this case is relatively easy and uncomplicated. Marriage forms also reflect the individual's life cycle. Most opt for free unions when they are younger and then settle into more formal marriages as they grow older and enjoy more economic security. Class also plays a role: religious marriage is favored by middle-class and upper-class groups; thus, it signifies higher socioeconomic status. The ideal marriage for most Hondurans involves a formal engagement and religious wedding, followed by an elaborate fiesta.

No shame accrues to the man who fathers many children and maintains several women as mistresses. Public disapproval follows only if the man fails to assume the role of "head of the family" and to support his children. When a free union dissolves, a woman typically receives only the house that she and her mate inhabited. The children receive support only if they have been legally recognized by their father.

Families are usually more stable in the countryside. Since the partners are usually residing in the midst of their kin, a man cannot desert his wife without disrupting his work relationship with her family. A woman enjoys greater leverage when she can rely on her family to assist if a union fails or when she owns her own land and thus has a measure of financial independence.

In keeping with the tradition of machismo, males usually play a dominant role within the family, and they receive the deference due to the head of the household. There is wide variation in practice, however. Where a man is absent, has limited economic assets, or is simply unassertive, a woman assumes the role of head of the family.

Sex role differentiation begins early: young boys are allowed to run about unclothed, while girls are much more carefully groomed and dressed. Bands of boys play unwatched; girls are carefully chaperoned. Girls are expected to be quiet and helpful; boys enjoy much greater freedom, and they are given considerable latitude in their behavior. Boys and men are expected to have premarital and extramarital sexual adventures. Men expect, however, that their brides be virgins. Parents go to considerable lengths to shelter their daughters in order to protect their chances of making a favorable marriage.

Parent-child relationships are markedly different depending on the sex of the parent. Mothers openly display affection for their children; the mother-child tie is virtually inviolate. Father-child relationships vary more depending on the family. Ideally, the father is an authority figure to be obeyed and respected; however, fathers are typically more removed from daily family affairs than mothers.

Living Conditions

Rural Life

Because Honduras has traditionally been an agrarian country and, in spite of rapid rates of urban growth, is still one of the least urbanized countries of Central America, conditions of life in the countryside are a major concern. Rural residents are farmers, although about 60 percent of Honduran land remains forested and only 25 percent of the total is available for agriculture or pastureland. A vast majority of rural dwellers are small farmers who till their own plots or landless laborers who work for wages on estates or smaller farms. Many peasants with plots of their own also seek part-time wage labor to supplement their incomes. In a typical case, a man may work his father's land, rent additional land of his own, and do occasional day labor.

The trend toward small farms in marginal areas increased rapidly after 1960 as the population increased explosively. Because land inheritance among the peasantry is divided among all the sons, a farmer with six *manzanas* (one *manzana* equals approximately 0.7 hectare) of land and six sons would have only one *manzana* of land for each child to work as his own as an adult. In addition, escalating land prices have increasingly forced small farmers to migrate to more and more marginal land because of population pressure and the rapid development of commercial agriculture and livestock estates since World War II. The steepness of the marginal mountain slopes, however, often makes agriculture impossible or at least extremely difficult. It is estimated that almost 90 percent of the mountainous area of Honduras has slopes with gradients that range from marginal for agriculture to those that do not permit agriculture or even decent pasturage. Obviously, small farmers attempting to cultivate the mountainsides have a difficult task.

Deterioration of the mountain environment, poor productivity, and crop losses result in poverty for small farmers. Soil erosion and the loss of soil fertility is caused by the marginality of the available slopes and the methods used in farming. Cultivation techniques are slash-and-mulch or slash-and-burn employing simple tools, such as machetes, hoes, axes, digging sticks, and possibly wooden plows, without the use of fertilizer. The rudimentary storage facilities of most farm households also contribute to the loss of a sizable percentage of crops to rodents and pests.

Most of the rural population live in one- or two-room thatchroofed huts (*bahareques*) built of adobe or sugarcane stalks and mud with dirt floors. As plantation agriculture and livestock raising have increased, many peasants have found it increasingly difficult to find a plot of land suitable for a house. Many who formerly lived on the edges of larger estates found themselves forced off the land by enclosure, or the fencing off of private property. Consequently, there is much "fence housing" in Honduras, in which a squatter and his family, squeezed off land by the development of plantation crops, live in a tiny hut in the narrow space between a public road and the landowner's fence.

Poor food productivity and low incomes lead to a very low standard of living in the countryside, where illness and poor diets are endemic. The typical diet of the rural population consists of corn by far the primary staple and most widely planted crop made into tortillas, beans the main source of protein cassava, plantains, rice, and coffee, with only occasional supplements of meat or fish. Although pigs and chickens are widely raised (each rural household usually has a few), meat is infrequent in most rural diets, as are green vegetables. Given the nature of the typical diet and the fact that food production has been insufficient for the country's needs, widespread malnutrition complicates the population's fragile health. Population growth exacerbates the problem, creating a vicious cycle of more mouths to be fed, yet lower agricultural productivity, as well as transportation and distribution difficulties.

Indeed, a general attitude has evolved in which most of the affected population has related few of its health problems to their real causes, such as malnutrition and environmental hazards. Instead, given a state of affairs where, for example, there is not a dramatic shortage of food but only a continuously inadequate diet, the population fails to relate infectious diseases, mental retardation, and low productivity to conditions of poor diet and lack of sanitation. Because these problems have always existed for the affected population, they tend to be accepted as normal.

Urban Life

Urban life in Honduras, as in many developing countries, highlights the contrasts between the life-styles of the rich and the poor. For the wealthy and powerful elite, Tegucigalpa and San Pedro Sula offer blocks of elegant apparel shops and jewelry stores. Tall office buildings provide headquarters for business and professional people. Comfortable homes shelter well-to-do families; a good education and family contacts secure promising future careers for their children.

For the vast majority of Tegucigalpa's urban population, however, living conditions are dismal. Migrants to Tegucigalpa initially settled in the slums of the center city. When these became inadequate to house the numbers arriving, the migrants began to invade land on the periphery of the city. A majority of these barrio residents live in *cuarterías* (rows) of connected rooms. Some *cuarterías* face the street, while others are arranged in double rows facing each other across a block-long alley, barely wide enough for a person to walk through. Usually windowless, the substandard rooms are generally constructed of wood, with dirt floors. The average household contains about seven persons, who attend to all functions of daily living in the single room, although sometimes a small kitchen stands in the rear covered by the overhang of the tile roof. For those living in the rooms facing an alley, the narrow passageway between buildings serves both as a sewage and waste disposal area and as a courtyard for as many as 150 persons.

The major survival tactic for some of this population seems to lie in the large and extended families that deliberately cluster together into a single room, sharing a roof, a kitchen, and their incomes. Both relatives and unrelated individuals may be involved in such a network of social, psychological, and economic support. Others, however, have not been so fortunate. Given migratory labor, high unemployment, and income insecurity, male-female relationships often are unstable. Fathers frequently desert their families, leaving the care and support of children entirely to mothers who struggle to earn enough for survival. Some children are abandoned to live on the streets, particularly if the mother has become sick, has died, or has been unable to find work.

The diet of lower-sector urban dwellers when they can afford to buy what they need is somewhat better than that of their rural counterparts. In times of economic hardship, however, urban families, who must pay for all the food they consume, most likely reduce or alter their food consumption habits. Speaking of a potentially better diet in urban areas can, therefore, be misleading. When urban families have the cash to purchase basic foods, their per capita daily average consumption of calories, protein, and carbohydrates are all likely to be higher than the average in rural settings. However, the consumption of calories, and carbohydrates in particular, still falls significantly below the minimum daily recommended allowance. Other foods sold mainly in city markets, especially meat such as poultry, are consumed primarily by the middle- and upper-class population and do not benefit the lower class.

Ethnic Groups

Around 90 percent of the population in Honduras is racially mestizo (people of mixed indigenous and European ancestry). The remainder of the population is composed of indigenous natives (7 percent); people of African descent, or blacks (2 percent); and those of European descent, or whites (1 percent). Mestizos, whites, and most blacks are culturally ladinos (those who practice Hispanic cultural patterns). Ladinos speak Spanish, and the majority are members of the Roman Catholic Church, although Protestant denominations made significant gains in membership among this group in the 1980s, especially in the larger cities.

Indigenous Groups

The Lenca, the largest indigenous group (numbering about 50,000), live in the west and in the southwestern interior. Some anthropologists argue that the Lenca still practice some traditional customs and that they are the survivors of a once extensive indigenous population that lived in the departments of Lempira, Intibucá, La Paz, Valle, Comayagua, and Francisco Morazán. Controversy has arisen, however, regarding the identification of this community as indigenous because their native language is no longer spoken and their culture is to a large extent similar to the ladino majority.

Other smaller indigenous groups are scattered throughout Honduras. Several hundred Chortí, a lowland Maya community, formerly lived in the departments of Copán and Ocotepeque in western Honduras. In the seventeenth and eighteenth centuries, the Chortí migrated to the northeast coastal area, and by the early 1990s, they were practically extinct. The Chorotega migrated south from Mexico in pre-Columbian times and settled in the department of Choluteca. Like the Chortí, the Chorotega speak Spanish, but they retain distinct cultural and religious traits. A population of Maya live in the western departments of Copán and Ocotepeque and still speak a Mayan dialect. Several hundred Pipil live mainly in the isolated northeast coastal region in the departments of Gracias a Dios and parts of Yoro and Olancho. About 300 Tol or Hicaque are found in an isolated mountainous area of rain forests.

Non-Ladino Groups

The non-Hispanic (nonladino) groups in Honduras consist of the Black Carib, the Miskito, the black population in the Islas de la Bahía, and a sizeable number of Arab immigrants. The Black Carib (also known as Garifuna in Belize and Guatemala) settled in the early 1800s in coastal villages along the Caribbean. Originally descendants of freed black slaves and native Carib from the island of Saint Vincent in the Caribbean, they arrived in Honduras when they were deported from Saint Vincent by the British in 1797 and resettled in the Islas de la Bahía off the coast of Honduras. From there, they moved to the mainland coast of northern Honduras. Their language, which they continue to speak, is a Carib-based creole. Their cultural practices are similar to those of the Black Carib who live in Belize and Guatemala.

The approximately 10,000 Miskito are a racially mixed population of indigenous, African, and European origin. Their language, still spoken by several thousand, is a creole based on Bahwika (in the Misumalpan family of languages), with contributions from West African languages as well as Spanish, English, and German. Spain's failure to conquer and colonize the eastern Caribbean lowlands of Central America made this area attractive to English-speaking buccaneers, traders, woodcutters, and planters during the seventeenth and eighteenth centuries. This remote area also became a refuge for black slaves and freed slaves. In the northern coasts of Honduras and Nicaragua, unions of indigenous people and the African and British immigrants produced a racially mixed group known as Miskito, who have a predominantly indigenous language and culture. Miskito settlements are situated near the Laguna de Caratasca and the banks of the Río Patuca in northeasternmost Honduras and are an extension of the larger Miskito communities in eastern Nicaragua. When the Nicaraguan Miskito population near the Río Coco was uprooted by the Nicaraguan government for security reasons in the early 1980s, many Nicaraguan Miskito migrated to Honduras.

Interestingly, although the Miskito and Black Carib peoples have similar racial origins, the Miskito are generally considered by Hondurans to be indigenous people, whereas the Black Carib are generally considered to be black. This difference in ethnic identification is probably a reflection of the different cultures of the two groups; Black Carib culture retains more African elements in its folklore, religion, and music than does the culture of the Miskito.

The Miskito and Black Carib peoples have traditionally been economically self-sufficient through subsistence agriculture and fishing. In the early 1990s, the men, however, were often forced to seek supplementary income by working outside their own regions. Thus, Miskito and Black Carib men often spend long periods separated from their families.

The population of the Islas de la Bahía is a black or mixed white-black population. The inhabitants are descendants of Englishspeaking whites and of blacks who came from Belize and the Cayman Islands during the middle of the nineteenth century. This population speaks mostly creole or Caribbean English, and their traditions are distinctly West Indian.

Another distinct ethnic group is the thriving Arab community. Arab immigrants from the Middle East (especially Palestine and Lebanon) began arriving in Honduras during the early part of the twentieth century. Because they held passports issued by the Ottoman Empire, they came to be called *turcos* in Honduras. This community retains many of its traditions and continues to be perceived as culturally distinct, although this distinctiveness is becoming blurred through increased intermarriages with other groups. Economically, the Arab community prospered first as merchants in the area of the banana plantations on the Caribbean coast. Following their success, many moved to the larger cities, where they became powerful economically, especially in manufacturing and commerce.

Religion

The constitution guarantees religious freedom and the separation of church and state; however, the Roman Catholic Church has been a powerful institution in Honduras since colonial times. As a result of various tensions between the church and the state throughout the centuries, in the 1880s the Roman Catholic Church was stripped of some of its economic and political power. Nevertheless, in the twentieth century the church has remained an important social actor, and the vast majority of Hondurans have remained Roman Catholic. Church schools receive government subsidies, and religious instruction is part of the public school curriculum.

The Roman Catholic Church in Honduras launched an ambitious evangelical campaign in the 1950s. The program's aim was to invigorate church membership and encourage more active participation in church activities. By the 1960s and 1970s, this activism had grown among certain sectors of the church into denunciations of the military's repression and the government's exploitation of the poor. This social activist phase in the Roman Catholic Church ended after large landowners in Olancho brutally murdered ten peasants, two students, and two priests in 1975. After this incident, the government took measures to dissuade the more activist factions in the church from continuing their actions. Expulsions and arrests of foreign priests took place, and some peasant centers with ties to the church were forced to close. The Roman Catholic Church retreated from its emphasis on social activism during the last half of the 1970s but resumed its criticism of government policies during the 1980s.

Protestant, especially evangelical, churches have undergone a tremendous growth in membership during the 1980s. The largest numbers are found in Methodist, Church of God, Seventh Day Adventist, and Assemblies of God denominations. These churches sponsor social service programs in many communities, making them attractive to the lower classes. The evangelical leadership generally exerts a conservative influence on the political process.

Although Protestant membership was estimated at only 100,000 in 1990, growth of Protestant churches is apparently seen as a threat by Roman Catholic leaders. Instances of criticism leveled at evangelicals by Roman Catholic leaders have increased; however, such criticisms have generally been ineffective in stemming the rise of converts to Protestant denominations.

Education

Honduras lacked a national education system until the late 1950s. Before the reforms of 1957, education was the exclusive privilege of those who could afford to send their children to private institutions. The government of Ramón Villeda Morales (1957-63) introduced reforms that led to the establishment of a national public education system and began a school construction program.

The Honduran constitution states that a free primary education is obligatory for every child between the ages of seven and fourteen. The reality of the Honduran educational system is much more grim. Because of a lack of schools, understaffed schools, the high cost of materials needed for these schools, and the poor quality of public education, a good education is still largely the privilege of the few who can afford to send their children to private institutions.

Statistical information shows that the state of the public education system remains poor. Figures cited by the Ministry of Education suggest that Honduras suffers from widespread illiteracy (more than 40 percent of the total population and more than 80 percent in rural areas). A significant percentage of children do not receive formal education. Especially in rural areas, schools are not readily accessible. When they are accessible, they often consist of joint-grade instruction through only the third grade. Schools are so understaffed that some teachers have up to eighty children in one classroom.

Only 43 percent of children enrolled in public schools complete the primary level. Of all children entering the first grade, only 30 percent go on to secondary school, and only 8 percent continue to the university.

The quality of instruction in Honduran public schools is greatly impaired by poor teacher training. The situation is worsened by the extremely low wages paid to teachers, lack of effective and up-to- date instruction materials, outdated teaching methods, poor administration, and lack of physical facilities.

Because of the deficiencies of public education, the years since 1970 have seen the proliferation of private schools. With few exceptions, however, private education is popularly viewed as a profit-making enterprise. Great skepticism remains regarding the quality of the education that private schools offer.

The National Autonomous University of Honduras (Universidad Nacional Autónoma de Honduras UNAH) is the primary institution of higher learning. Located in Tegucigalpa, the UNAH was founded in 1847 and became an autonomous institution in 1957. The university has approximately 30,000 students, with branches in San Pedro Sula and La Ceiba.

Honduras counts three private universities, none of which is yet considered a credible educational alternative to the prestigious UNAH. One is the extremely small José Cecilio del Valle University in Tegucigalpa. Another private university is the Central American Technological University, also in Tegucigalpa. The third private university is the University of San Pedro Sula.

Health

In Honduras the quality of and access to health care are directly tied to income levels. Adequate health care is available to those able to pay the high cost. Health care for the urban and rural poor is extremely limited. The lack of health care for the majority of the population is starkly apparent in its poor health. Widespread malnutrition is responsible for 34 percent of children experiencing stunting when they are between two and five years of age. In addition, most of the population lacks access to running water and sanitation facilities all key contributing factors to the country's high infant mortality rate (63 per 1,000 live births) and to a relatively low life expectancy rate (64.9 years) in 1992.

Health services are not readily accessible to a majority of the population. An estimated 1.3 million Hondurans were without access to health care in 1990. In the isolated regions of Honduras, there are almost no physicians. The ratio of doctor to population in 1984 was one to 1,510. Government clinics often are empty shells lacking adequate personnel, equipment, and medicines.

Infectious and parasitic diseases are the leading causes of death. Gastroenteritis and tuberculosis are serious problems. Diseases such as influenza, malaria, typhoid, and pneumonia, once believed to be under control, have returned in force because of a lack of preventive measures. The foreign-exchange crisis of the 1980s has resulted in periods when vaccines and other preventive medicines were not available. Alcoholism and drug addiction are other health concerns mentioned by the Ministry of Health. The rapid spread of acquired immune deficiency syndrome (AIDS) is also of great concern to Honduran health authorities. The incidence of AIDS appears to be particularly high in San Pedro Sula.

The cholera epidemic that originated in Peru hit Honduras in late 1991. Because of poor sanitation conditions, health officials were frightened that the disease would quickly spread throughout the country. The government launched an educational campaign months before the first case was reported, stressing personal hygiene as a prophylaxis against cholera. By the middle of 1992, however, more than 100 people had been diagnosed as having cholera.

Although the country's national public health system was created in 1959, the date when the Honduran Social Security Institute (Instituto Hondureño del Seguro Social IHSS) began to operate, the proliferation of health services to all regions of the country has been painfully slow. For years, people have had to travel to Tegucigalpa to avail themselves of public health service. During the 1970s, when the government made an effort to expand health services, the INSS opened a medical center in San Pedro Sula. However, in El Progreso, only fifty kilometers away and the third largest city in the country, IHSS services were not available until 1992. Population growth, the implementation of economic austerity measures by the government in the 1990s, and the present lack of facilities seem to suggest that public health services in Honduras are likely to remain inadequate in the near future.

The Environment

The 1980s saw a heightened awareness and concern over ecological issues. Even though Honduras is not overpopulated, its land resources have been overexploited, and there are numerous reasons for concern regarding deforestation and the prevalence of unsustainable agricultural practices. Enforcement of the few regulations already in effect is uneven.

Honduras has two major national parks. One is the Tigra Cloud Forest Park near Tegucigalpa. The other is the Copán National Park near the border with Guatemala, which houses the Mayan ruins. Honduras also has established the Río Plátano Reserve. Furthermore, the government has attempted to encourage ecotourism in the Islas de la Bahía, where biologically rich coral reefs are located.

As a consequence of the expansion of environmental consciousness, the Honduran Association of Ecology (Asociación Hondureña de la Ecología AHE) was founded in the 1980s. Following the example set in the foundation of the AHE, many other groups formed with the stated purpose of promoting ecologically sound policies. Unfortunately, in 1993 many sources of international funding dried up following the discovery of corruption in a number of Honduran ecological groups. Despite the continued presence of many environmental problems, ecologists are encouraged by the increasing environmental consciousness among all sectors of the population. The fact that environmental concerns are part of the policies advocated by peasant organizations, labor unions, and other interest groups is a sign that the ecological movement has come to maturity.

Honduran society provides examples of the most severe problems faced by developing nations. Yet within that same society, the unique relationship between social and political forces provides potential for progress in alleviating the country's problems.

The Economy

Honduras was one of the poorest countries in the Western Hemisphere in 1993. Since colonial times, the Honduran economy has been built mostly on one commodity—minerals before to 1900 and bananas during the first half of the twentieth century. The Honduran economy is dependent on international pricing for its principal export commodity, as is true for most impoverished nations whose survival is based on a single export item. Despite efforts to diversify agriculture, bananas remained the nation's principal export in the early 1990s, leaving the country vulnerable to market changes. The government has sought to invigorate the industrial sector and increase assembly activities, but these measures have had very limited success. As a result, the nation continues to lack a reliable source of economic development.

Honduras' economic growth is hampered by a lack of resources, fertile land, and a tiny local market. Most notably, Honduras lacks rich natural resources, with only land seeming to be abundant and easily exploited. However, the seeming abundance of land is deceptive since the country's rough, hilly geography limits large-scale agricultural production to limited strips along the coastlines and a few fertile valleys. Honduras' industrial industry has struggled to go beyond basic textile and agricultural processing businesses, as well as assembly activities. The region's tiny domestic market and competition from more industrially advanced nations have stifled more complicated industrialisation.

Growth and Structure of the Economy

After Honduras achieved independence from Spain in the early nineteenth century, its economic growth became closely related to its ability to develop attractive export products. During much of the nineteenth century, the Honduran economy languished;

traditional cattle raising and subsistence agriculture produced no suitable major export. In the latter part of the century, economic activity quickened with the development of large-scale, preciousmetal mining. The most important mines were located in the mountains near the capital of Tegucigalpa and were owned by the New York and Honduras Rosario Mining Company (NYHRMC). Silver was the principal metal extracted, accounting for about 55 percent of exports in the 1880s. Mining income stimulated commercial and ancillary enterprises, built some infrastructure, and reduced monetary restraints on trade. Other beneficial economic effects were few, however, because the mining industry was never well integrated into the rest of the Honduran economy. The foreign mining companies employed a small work force, provided little or no government revenue, and relied mostly on imported mining equipment.

Honduras's international economic activity surged in the early twentieth century. Between 1913 and 1929, its agricultural exports rose from US$3 million (US$2 million from bananas) to US$25 million (US$21 million from bananas). These "golden" exports were supported by more than US$40 million of specialized banana company investment in the Honduran infrastructure and were safeguarded by United States pressure on the national government when the companies felt threatened.

The overall performance of the Honduran economy remained closely tied to banana prices and production from the 1920s until after the mid-century because other forms of commercial export agriculture were slow to emerge. In addition, until drastically reduced in the mid-1950s, the work force associated with banana cultivation represented a significant proportion of the wage earners in the country. Just before the banana industry's largest strike in 1954, approximately 35,000 workers held jobs on the banana plantations of the United Fruit Company (later United Brands Company, then Chiquita Brands International) or the Standard Fruit

Company (later brought by Castle and Cook, then Dole Food Company).

After 1950 Honduran governments encouraged agricultural modernization and export diversification by spending heavily on transportation and communications infrastructure, agricultural credit, and technical assistance. During the 1950s as a result of these improvements and the strong international export prices beef, cotton, and coffee became significant export products for the first time. Honduran sugar, timber, and tobacco also were exported, and by 1960 bananas had declined to a more modest share (45 percent) of total exports. During the 1960s, industrial growth was stimulated by the establishment of the Central American Common Market (CACM see Appendix B). As a result of the reduction of regional trade barriers and the construction of a high common external tariff, some Honduran manufactured products, such as soaps, sold successfully in other Central American countries. Because of the greater size and relative efficiency of the Salvadoran and Guatemalan industrial sectors, however, Honduras bought far more manufactured products from its neighbors than it sold to them. After the 1969 Soccer War with El Salvador, Honduras effectively withdrew from the CACM. Favorable bilateral trade arrangements between Honduras and the other former CACM partners were subsequently negotiated, however.

A political shift in the 1980s had strong and unexpected repercussions on the country's economic condition. Beginning in late 1979, as insurgency spread in neighboring countries, Honduran military leaders enthusiastically came to support United States policies in the region. This alignment resulted in financial support that benefited the civilian as well as the military ministries and agencies of Honduras. Honduran defense spending rose throughout the 1980s until it consumed 20 to 30 percent of the national budget. Before the military buildup began in fiscal year (FY) 1980, United States military assistance to Honduras was less than US$4 million. Military aid more than doubled to reach just under US$9 million by

FY 1981, surged to more than US$31 million by FY 1982, and stood at US$48.3 million in FY 1983. Tiny Honduras soon became the tenth largest recipient of United States assistance aid; total economic and military aid rose to more than US$200 million in 1985 and remained at more than US$100 million for the rest of the 1980s.

The increasing dependence of the Honduran economy on foreign aid was aggravated by a severe, regionwide economic decline during the 1980s. Private investment plummeted in 1980, and capital flight for that year was US$500 million. To make matters worse, coffee prices plunged on the international market in the mid-1980s and remained low throughout the decade. In 1993 average annual per capita income remained depressingly low at about US$580, and 75 percent of the population was poor by internationally defined standards.

Traditionally, Honduran economic hopes have been pinned on land and agricultural commodities. Despite those hopes, however, usable land has always been severely limited. Honduras's mostly mountainous terrain confines agriculturally exploitable land to narrow bands along the coasts and to some previously fertile but now largely depleted valleys. The country's once abundant forest resources have also been dramatically reduced, and Honduras has not derived economically significant income from mineral resources since the nineteenth century. Similarly, Honduras's industrial sector never was fully developed. The heady days of the CACM (midto - late 1960s), which produced an industrial boom for El Salvador and Guatemala, barely touched the Honduran economy except to increase its imports because of the comparative advantages enjoyed by the Salvadoran and Guatemalan economies and Honduras's inability to compete.

Bananas and coffee have also proven unreliable sources of income. Although bananas are less subject to the vagaries of international markets than coffee, natural disasters such as Hurricane Fifi in 1974, drought, and disease have appeared with a regular, albeit random, frequency to take their economic toll through severely diminished harvests. Moreover, bananas are grown and marketed mostly by international corporations, which keep the bulk of wealth generated. Coffee exports, equally unreliable as a major source of economic support, surpassed bananas in the mid1970s as Honduras's leading export income earner, but international price declines coupled with huge fiscal deficits underlined the vulnerability of coffee as an economic base.

As Honduras entered the 1990s, it did have some factors working in its favor relative peace and a stronger civilian government with less military interference in the politics and economy of the country than in past years. The country was hobbled, however, by horrendous foreign debt, could claim only diminished natural resources, and had one of the fastest growing and urbanizing populations in the world. The government's daunting task then became how to create an economic base able to compensate for the withdrawal of much United States assistance without becoming solely dependent on traditional agricultural exports.

In the 1990s, bananas were booming again, particularly as new European trade agreements increased market size. Small bananaproducing cooperatives lined up in the 1990s to sell their land to the commercial giants, and the last banana-producing lands held by the government were privatized. Like most of Central America, Honduras in the 1990s began to woo foreign investors, mostly Asian clothing assembly firms, and it held high hopes for revenue to be generated by privatizing national industries. With one of the most strikeprone labor forces in Central America, debt-burdened and aging industrial assets, and a dramatically underdeveloped infrastructure, Honduras, however, has distinct economic disadvantages relative to its Central American and Caribbean neighbors, who compete with Honduras in the same export markets.

Macroeconomic Trends

Recent Growth

Honduran president Rafael Leonardo Callejas Romero, elected in November 1989, enjoyed little success in the early part of his administration as he attempted to adhere to a standard economic austerity package prescribed by the International Monetary Fund (IMF) and the World Bank. As the November 1993 presidential elections drew closer, the political fallout of austere economic measures made their implementation even less likely. Any hope for his party's winning the 1993 election was predicated on improving social programs, addressing employment needs, and appeasing a disgruntled, vocal public sector. However, reaching those goals required policies that moved away from balancing the budget, lowering inflation, and reducing the deficit and external debt to attract investment and stimulate economic growth.

Callejas inherited an economic mess. The economy had deteriorated rapidly, starting in 1989, as the United States Agency for International Development (AID) pointedly interrupted disbursements of its grants to Honduras to signal displeasure with the economic policies of the old government and to push the new government to make economic reforms. Nondisbursal of those funds greatly exacerbated the country's economic problems. Funds from the multilateral lending institutions, which eventually would help fill the gap left by the reduction of United States aid, were still under negotiation in 1989 and would be conditioned first on payment of arrears on the country's enormous external debt.

Between 1983 and 1985, the government of Honduras pumped up by massive infusions of external borrowing had introduced expensive, high-tech infrastructure projects. The construction of roads and dams, financed mostly by multilateral loans and grants, was intended to generate employment to compensate for the impact of the regionwide recession. In reality, the development projects served to swell the ranks of public-sector employment and line the pockets of a small elite. The projects never sparked private-sector investment or created substantial private employment. Instead, per capita income continued to fall as

Honduras's external debt doubled. Even greater injections of foreign assistance between 1985 and 1988 kept the economy afloat, but it soon became clear that the successive governments had been borrowing time as well as money.

Foreign aid between 1985 and 1989 represented about 4.6 percent of the gross domestic product (GDP). About 44 percent of the government's fiscal shortfall was financed through cash from foreign sources. Side effects of the cash infusion were that the national currency, the lempira became overvalued and the amount of exports dropped. A booming public sector, with its enhanced ability to import, was enough to keep the economy showing growth, based on private consumption and government spending. But the government did little to address the historical, underlying structural problems of the economy its overdependence on too few traditional commodities and lack of investment. Unemployment mushroomed, and private investment withered.

By 1989 President Callejas's broad economic goal became to return Honduran economic growth to 1960-80 levels. During the decades of the 1960s and 1970s, the country's economy, spurred mostly by erratically fluctuating traditional agricultural commodities, nevertheless averaged real annual growth of between 4 and 5 percent. At the end of the 1980s, however, Callejas had few remaining vehicles with which to pull the country out of the deep regionwide recession of the 1980s. Real growth between 1989 and 1993 translated to mostly negative or small positive per capita changes in the GDP for a population that was growing at close to 4 percent annually.

President Callejas attempted to adhere to conditions of desperately needed new loans. Cutting the size of the public sector work force, lowering the deficit, and enhancing revenues from taxes as mandated by the multilateral lending institutions were consistently his biggest stumbling blocks. Despite his all-out effort to reduce the public-sector deficit, the overall ratio of fiscal deficit to the GDP in 1990 showed little change from that in 1989. The total public-sector deficit actually grew to 8.6 percent of the GDP, or nearly L1 billion, in 1991. The 1993 deficit expanded to 10.6 percent of the GDP. The Honduran government's medium-term economic objectives, as dictated by the IMF, were to have generated real GDP growth of 3.5 percent by 1992 and 4 percent by 1993. In fact, GDP growth was 3.3 percent in 1991, 5.6 percent in 1992, and an estimated 3.7 percent in 1993. The economy had operated so long on an ad hoc basis that it lacked the tools to implement coherent economic objectives. Solving the most immediate crisis frequently took precedence over long-term goals.

Inflation

By 1991 President Callejas had achieved modest success in controlling inflation. Overall inflation for 1990 had reached 36.4 percent not the hyperinflation experienced by some Latin American counties but still the highest annual rate for Honduras in forty years. The Honduran government and the IMF had set an inflation target of 12 percent for 1992 and 8 percent for 1993. The actual figures were 8.8 percent in 1992 and an estimated 10.7 percent for 1993. Hondurans had been accustomed to low inflation (3.4 percent in 1985, rising to 4.5 percent by the end of 1986), partly because pegging the lempira to the dollar linked Honduras's inflation rate to inflation rates in developed countries. But the expectation for low inflation made the reality of high inflation that much worse and created additional pressures on the government for action when inflation soared in 1990.

Unemployment

Between 1980 and 1983, 20 percent of the work force was unemployed double the percentage of the late 1970s. Job creation remained substantially behind the growth of the labor force throughout the 1980s. Unemployment grew to 25 percent by 1985, and combined unemployment and underemployment jumped to 40 percent in 1989. By 1993, 50 to 60 percent of the Honduran labor force was estimated to be either underemployed or unemployed.

The government's acceptance of foreign aid during the 1980s, in lieu of economic growth sparked by private investment, allowed it to ignore the necessity of creating new jobs. Honduras's GDP showed reasonable growth throughout most of the 1980s, especially when compared to the rest of Latin America, but it was artificially buoyed by private consumption and public-sector spending.

Mainstay agricultural jobs became scarcer in the late 1970s. Coffee harvests and plantings in border area decreased because fighting in neighboring Nicaragua and El Salvador spilled over into Honduran. Other factors contributing to the job scarcity were limited land, a reluctance on the part of coffee growers to invest while wars destabilized the region, and a lack of credit. Small farmers became increasingly unable to support themselves as their parcels of land diminished in size and productivity.

Problems in the agricultural sector have fueled urbanization. The Honduran population was 77 percent rural in 1960. By 1992 only 55 percent of the Honduran population continued to live in rural areas. Campesinos have flocked to the cities in search of work but found little there. Overall unemployment has been exacerbated by an influx of refugees from the wars in neighboring countries, attracted to Honduras, ironically, by its relatively low population density and relative peace. In the agricultural sector (which in 1993 still accounted for approximately 60 percent of the labor force), unemployment has been estimated to be far worse than the figures for the total labor force.

Honduran urban employment in the early 1990s has been characterized by underemployment and marginal informal-sector jobs, as thousands of former agricultural workers and refugees have moved to the cities seeking better lives. Few new jobs have been generated in the formal sector, however, because domestic private sector and foreign investment has dropped and coveted public-sector jobs have been reserved mostly for the small Honduran middle-class with political or military connections. Only one of ten Honduran workers was securely employed in the formal sector in 1991.

In the mid-1980s, the World Bank reported that only 10,000 new jobs were created annually; the low rate of job creation resulted in 20,000 people being added to the ranks of the unemployed every year. The actual disparity between jobs needed for full employment and new jobs created exceeded that projection, however. For those with jobs, the buying power of their wages tumbled throughout the 1980s while the cost of basic goods, especially food, climbed precipitously.

Role of Government

Fiscal Policies

Throughout the 1960s and most of the 1970s, the military-led governments of Honduras ran a state-sponsored and state-financed economy. The governments provided most guarantees for loans to a strong but patronage-dominated and somewhat corrupt public sector that included recipients of graft extracted from foreign and domestic investors, and to costly state-developed enterprises. By 1989 and the election of President Callejas, however, a heavy toll had been taken by regionwide economic recession, civil war in neighboring countries, the drying up of most external credit, and capital flight equaling more than US$1.5 billion. Callejas began to shift economic policy toward privatizing government-owned enterprises, liberalizing trade and tariff regulations, and encouraging increased foreign investment through tax and other incentives. The Callejas administration did not seek less government control. Rather it changed the government's objectives by focusing on reducing public-sector spending, the size of the public-sector work force, and the trade deficit. Overall economic planning became the responsibility of the National Superior Planning Council, directed by the minister of economy and commerce. President Callejas, a United States-trained economist, brought new professionalism and technical skills to the central government as he began the arduous task of long-term economic reform.

Monetary and Exchange-Rate Policies

The official exchange rate of the lempira, pegged at US$1=L2 since 1918, was dramatically devalued in 1990. Exchange controls had been introduced in 1982, resulting in a parallel currency market (black market) and several confusing official exchange rates operating simultaneously. Some of those rates were legally recognized in 1990 when President Callejas introduced a major series of economic policy reforms, which included reducing the maximum import tariff rate from 90 percent to 40 percent and getting rid of most surcharges and exemptions. The value of the lempira was adjusted to US$1=L4, with the exception of the rate for debt equity conversions, which remained at the old rate of US$1=L2. The official conversion rate of the lempira fell to US$1=L7.26 in December 1993. The president also introduced temporary taxes on exports, which were intended to increase central government revenue. Additional price and trade liberalization measures and fewer government regulations became part of his ongoing reforms.

Budget

Throughout the 1980s, the Honduran government was heavily financed by foreign assistance. External financing mostly bilateral credit from the United States rose dramatically until it reached 87 percent of the public deficit in 1985, rising even further in subsequent years. By 1991 the public-sector deficit was entirely financed with net external credit. That financing permitted the government to reduce the demand for internal credit and, therefore, to maintain its established exchange rate.

In 1991 President Callejas managed to give the appearance of having reduced the overall fiscal deficit, a requirement for new credit. The deficit decrease, however, was mostly an accounting device because it resulted from the postponement of external payments to the Paris Club debtors and eventually would be offset by pressure to raise public investment. During 1991, loan negotiations with multilateral and bilateral lending institutions brought Honduras US$39.5 million in United States development assistance, US$70 million in balance-of-payments assistance in the form of cash grants, and US$18.8 million in food aid. The country also negotiated US$302.4 million in concessional loans from the multilateral lending institutions. Total outstanding external debt as a percentage of GDP fell from 119 percent in 1990 to 114 percent in 1991 and to 112 percent in 1993. This drop was largely the result of debt forgiveness of US$448.4 million by the United States, Switzerland, and the Netherlands. Scheduled amortization payments of an average US$223.2 million per year, however, guaranteed that Honduras's gross funding requirements would remain large indefinitely.

The government of Honduras projected that overall tax revenues would increase from 13.2 percent of GDP in 1989 to about 15.7 percent in 1991. Adjustments for low coffee prices and the continuation of lax collection methods, however, undermined those goals. Despite these tax increases, compared to developed countries, Honduras has low tax rates with particularly low property taxes.

Labor

Composition of Labor Force

Honduras suffers from an overabundance of unskilled and uneducated laborers. Most Honduran workers in 1993 continued to be employed in agriculture, which accounted for about 60 percent of the labor force. More than half of the rural population, moreover, remains landless and heavily dependent on diminishing seasonal labor and low wages. Fifty-five percent of the farming population subsists on less than two hectares and earns less than US$70 per capita per year from those plots, mostly by growing subsistence food crops.

In 1993 only about 9 to 13 percent of the Honduran labor force was engaged in the country's tiny manufacturing sector one of the smallest in Central America. Skilled laborers are scarce. Only 25,000 people per year, of which about 21 percent are industrial workers, graduate yearly from the National Institute of Professional Training (Instituto Nacional de Formación Profesional- -INFOP) established in 1972.

Hundreds of small manufacturing firms, the traditional backbone of Honduran enterprise, began to go out of business beginning in the early 1990s, as import costs rose and competition through increasing wages for skilled labor from the mostly Asian-owned assembly industries strengthened. The small Honduran shops, most of which had manufactured clothing or food products for the domestic market, traditionally received little support in the form of credit from the government or the private sector and were more like artisans than conventional manufacturers. Asian-owned export assembly firms (*maquiladoras*), operating mostly in free zones established by the government on the Caribbean coast, attract thousands of job seekers and swell the populations of new city centers such as San Pedro Sula, Tela, and La Ceiba. Those firms employed approximately 16,000 workers in 1991.

About one-third of the Honduran labor force was estimated to be working in the service or "other" sector in 1993. That classification usually means that a person ekes out a precarious livelihood in the urban informal sector or as a poorly paid domestic. As unemployment soared throughout Central America in the 1980s, more and more people were forced to rely on their own ingenuity in order to simply exist on the fringes of Honduran society.

Employment Indicators and Benefits

Honduran governments have set minimum wages since 1974, but enforcement has generally been lax. That laxity increased at the beginning of the 1980s. Traditionally, most Honduran workers have not been covered by social security, welfare, or minimum wages. Multinational companies usually paid more than the standard minimum wage, but, overall, the Honduran wage earner has experienced a diminution of real wages and purchasing ability for more than a decade. When they occurred, minimum wage adjustments generally did not keep up with cost of living increases. After a major currency devaluation in 1990, average Honduran workers were among the most poorly paid workers in the Western Hemisphere. By contrast, the banana companies paid relatively high wages as early as the 1970s. Banana workers continued at the top of the wage scale in the 1990s; however, in the 1980s, as banana production became less laborintensive , the companies had decreased their investment and work force. Consequently, fewer workers were employed as relatively well-paid agricultural wage earners with related benefits.

President Callejas responded to the severe poverty by implementing a specially financed Honduran Social Investment Fund (Fondo Hondureño de Inversión Social FHIS) in 1990. The fund created public works programs such as road maintenance and provided United States surplus food to mothers and infants. Many Hondurans slipped through that fragile social safety net, however. As a continuing part of the social pact, and even more as the result of a fierce union-government battle, President Callejas announced in 1991 a 27.8 percent increase over a minimum wage that the government had earlier agreed upon. That increase was in addition to raises of 50 and 22 percent set, respectively, in January and September 1990. Despite those concessions, the minimum daily rate in 1991 was only US$1.75 for workers employed by small agricultural enterprises and US$3.15 for workers in the big exporting concerns; most workers did not earn the minimum wage.

Labor Unions

Honduras has long been heavily unionized. In 1993 approximately 15 to 20 percent of the overall formal work force was represented by some type of union, and about 40 percent of urban workers were union members. There were forty-eight strikes in the public sector alone in 1990, protesting the government's economic austerity program and layoffs of public-sector workers. More than

4,000 public-sector employees from the Ministry of Communications, Public Works, and Transport were fired in 1990. About 70,000 unionized workers remained in the faltering public sector in the beginning of 1991. However, the government largely made good its pledge to trim that number by 8,000 to 10,000 throughout 1991 as part of its austerity program.

In the private sector, 1990 saw ninety-four strikes in sixtyfour firms as workers fought for wage increases to combat inflation. A forty-two-day strike at the Tela Railroad Company (owned by Chiquita Brands International formerly United Brands and United Fruit Company) was unsuccessful, however, and that defeat temporarily ended union efforts at direct confrontation.

In 1993 Honduras had three major labor confederations: the Confederation of Honduran Workers (Confederación de Trabajadores de Honduras CTH), claiming a membership of about 160,000 workers; the General Workers' Central (Central General de Trabajadores CGT), claiming to represent 120,000 members; and the Unitary Confederation of Honduran Workers (Confederación Unitaria de Trabajadores de Honduras CUTH), a new confederation formed in May 1992, with an estimated membership of about 30,000. The three confederations included numerous trade union federations, individual unions, and peasant organizations.

The CTH, the nation's largest trade confederation, was formed in 1964 by the nation's largest peasant organization, the National Association of Honduran Peasants (Asociación Nacional de Campesinos de Honduras Anach), and by Honduran unions affiliated with the Inter-American Regional Organization of Workers (Organización Regional Interamericana de Trabajadores ORIT), a hemispheric labor organization with close ties to the American Federation of LaborCongress of Industrial Organization (AFL-CIO). In the early 1990s, the confederation had three major components: the 45,000-member Federation of Unions of National Workers of Honduras (Federación Sindical de Trabajadores Nacionales de Honduras Fesitranh); the 22,000 member Central Federation of

Honduran Free Trade Unions (Federación Central de Sindicatos Libres de Honduras); and the 2,200-member Federation of National Maritime Unions of Honduras (Federación de Sindicales Marítimas Nacionales de Honduras). In addition, Anach, claiming to represent between 60,000 and 80,000 members, was affiliated with Fesitranh. Fesitranh was by far the country's most powerful labor federation, with most of its unions located in San Pedro Sula and the Puerto Cortés Free Zone. The unions of the United States-owned banana companies and the United States-owned petroleum refinery also were affiliated with Fesitranh. The CTH received support from foreign labor organizations, including ORIT, the American Institute for Free Labor Development (AIFLD), and Germany's Friedreich Ebert Foundation and was an affiliate of the International Confederation of Free Trade Unions (ICFTU).

Although it was not legally recognized until 1982, the CGT was originally formed in 1970 by the Christian Democrats and received external support from the World Confederation of Labor (WCL) and the Latin American Workers Central (Central Latinoamericana de Trabajadores CLAT), a regional organization supported by Christian Democratic parties. In the late 1980s and early 1990s, however, the CGT leadership developed close ties to the National Party of Honduras (Partido Nacional de Honduaras PNH), and several leaders served in the Callejas government. Another national peasant organization, the National Union of Peasants (Unión Nacional de Campesinos UNC), claiming a membership of 40,000, was affiliated with the CGT for many years and was a principal force within the confederation.

The CUTH was formed in May 1992 by two principal labor federations, the Unitary Federation of Honduran Workers (Federación Unitaria de Trabajadores de Honduras FUTH) and the Independent Federation of Honduran Workers (Federación Independiente de Trabajadores de Honduras FITH), as well as several smaller labor groups, all critical of the Callejas government's neoliberal economic reform program.

The Marxist FUTH, with an estimated 16,000 members in the early 1990s, was first organized in 1980 by three communist-influenced unions, but did not receive legal status until 1988. The federation had external ties with the World Federation of Trade Unions (WFTU), the Permanent Congress for Latin American Workers Trade Union Unity (Congreso Permanente de Unidad Sindical de Trabajadores de América Latina CPUSTAL), and the Central American Committee of Trade Union Unity (Comité de Unidad Sindical de Centroamérica CUSCA). Its affiliations included water utility, university, electricity company, brewery, and teacher unions, as well as several peasant organizations, including the National Central of Farm Workers (Central Nacional de Trabajadores del Campo CNTC), formed in 1985 and active in land occupations in the early 1980s.

FUTH also became affiliated with a number of leftist popular organizations in a group known as the Coordinating Committee of Popular Organizations (Comité Coordinadora de las Organizaciones Populares CCOP) that was formed in 1984. Dissident FUTH member formed the FITH, which was granted legal status in 1988. The FITH consisted of fourteen unions claiming about 13,000 members in the early 1990s.

Agriculture

Land Use

The total land area of Honduras is 11.2 million hectares, of which a scant 1.7 million hectares (about 15 percent) are well suited for agriculture. Most land in Honduras is covered by mountains, giving rise to the country's nickname, "the Tibet of Central America." Nevertheless, the Honduran economy has always depended almost exclusively on agriculture, and in 1992 agriculture was still the largest sector of the economy, contributing 28 percent to the GDP. Less than half of Honduras's cultivable land was planted with crops as recently as the mid-1980s. The rest was used for pastures or was forested and was owned by the government or the banana corporations. Potential for additional productivity from fallow land was questionable, however, because much of Honduras's soil lacks the thick volcanic ash found elsewhere in Central America. In addition, by 1987 about 750,000 hectares of Honduran land had been seriously eroded as a result of misuse by cattle ranchers and slash-and-burn squatters who planted unsuitable food crops.

The Honduran government and two banana companies Chiquita Brands International and Dole Food Company owned approximately 60 percent of Honduras's cultivable land in 1993. The banana companies acquired most of their landholdings in the early twentieth century in return for building the railroads used to transport bananas from the interior to the coast. Much of their land remained unused because it lacked irrigation. Only about 14 percent of cultivated land was irrigated in 1987. Most land under cultivation in 1992 was planted in bananas, coffee, and specialized export crops such as melons and winter vegetables.

Agricultural Policy

The agricultural sector's output showed little or no growth between 1970 and 1985. As a result of favorable weather and market conditions beginning in 1985, however, the agricultural sector grew at a rate of 2.6 percent annually, slightly above the average for Latin America during that period. Production of basic grains and coffee increased; the export price of bananas was high; and pork, poultry, and milk produced for the domestic market increased. Nontraditional fruits and vegetables also increased in value.

Honduran agricultural production overall has tended to be low because the amount of crop yielded by a given amount of land has been low. For example, Honduran coffee yields historically have been only about half those of Costa Rica. Instead of using improved techniques to increase the productivity of the land, Honduran farmers have merely expanded the hectarage under cultivation to produce more crops pushing their fields ever farther into the forests. Given the limited amount of good quality agricultural land to begin with, that policy has resulted in continual deforestation and subsequent erosion. This reluctance to improve techniques, coupled with generally poor soil, a lack of credit, and poor infrastructure, has contributed to low production figures.

Land Reform

The Honduran government nominally began to address inequitable land ownership in the early 1960s. Those efforts at reform focused on organizing rural cooperatives. About 1,500 hectares of government-owned land were distributed by the National Agrarian Institute (Instituto Nacional Agrario INA) beginning in 1960.

A military coup in 1963 resulted in an end to the land reform program. Lacking even modest government-directed land reforms, illegal squatting became the primary means for poor people to gain land throughout the early 1970s. These actions spurred the government to institute new agrarian reforms in 1972 and 1975. Although all lands planted in export crops were exempted from reform, about 120,000 hectares were, nevertheless, divided among 35,000 poor families.

By 1975 the pendulum had swung back, and agrarian reform was all but halted. From 1975 through the 1980s, illegal occupations of unused land increased once again. The need for land reform was addressed mostly by laws directed at granting titles to squatters and other landholders, permitting them to sell their land or to use it as collateral for loans.

Despite declarations by the Callejas government in 1989 of its intent to increasingly address social issues, including land tenure and other needs of small farmers, the early 1990s were jolted by increased conflicts between peasants and the Honduran security forces. Agricultural credit and government support increasingly favored export crop producers at the expense of producers of basic food crops.

The Honduran land reform process under President Callejas between 1989 and 1992 was directed primarily at large agricultural landowners. An agrarian pact, signed by landowners and peasant organizations in August 1990, remained underfunded and largely unimplemented. Furthermore, violence erupted as discharged members of the Honduran military forcibly tried to claim land that had already been awarded to the peasant organization Anach in 1976. In May 1991, violence initiated by members of the Honduran military resulted in the deaths of eight farmers. To keep similar situations around the country from escalating into violence, the government promised to parcel out land belonging to the National Corporation for Investment (Corporación Nacional de Inversiones Conadin). The government also pledged to return to peasants land that had been confiscated by the Honduran military in 1983.

An Agricultural Modernization Law, passed in 1992, accelerated land titling and altered the structure of land cooperatives formed in the 1960s. The law permitted cooperative members to break up their holdings into small personal plots that could be sold. As a result, some small banana producers suffering from economic hard times chose to sell their land to the giant banana producers. After an agreement was reached with the European Union (EU) to increase Honduras's banana quota to the EU, the large banana companies were avid for additional land for increased production to meet the anticipated new demand from Europe.

Traditional Crops

Throughout the twentieth century, Honduras's agriculture has been dominated first by bananas and then to a lesser extent by coffee and sugar. Although their overall importance has declined somewhat, bananas and coffee together still accounted for 50 percent of the value of Honduran exports in 1992. The combined value of the two crops also continued to make the biggest contribution to the economy in 1992. Total banana sales that year were US$287 million, and total coffee sales amounted to US$148 million. These figures, which reflect a substantial decline from previous years' sales, reflect production losses suffered by banana producers and the withholding of coffee exports from the market in a futile effort to force improvements in the face of record breaking price declines.

Two United States-based, multinational corporations Chiquita Brands International and Dole Food Company now account for most Honduran banana production and exports. Honduras's traditional system of independent banana producers, who, as late as the 1980s, sold their crops to the international banana companies, was eroded in the 1990s. In the absence of policies designed to protect independent suppliers, economically strapped cooperatives began to sell land to the two large corporations.

Although Honduran banana production is dominated by multinational giants, such is not the case with coffee, which is grown by about 55,000 mostly small producers. Coffee production in Honduras has been high despite relatively low yields because of the large numbers of producers. Honduras, in fact, consistently produced more than its international quota until growers began to withhold the crop in the 1980s in an attempt to stimulate higher prices. Despite the efforts of the growers, coffee prices plunged on the international market from a high of more than US$2.25 per kilogram in the mid-1970s to less than US$0.45 per kilogram in the early 1990s. As a result of the declining prices, coffee producers were becoming increasingly marginalized.

The outlook for the sugar industry, which had boomed during the 1980s when Honduran producers were allowed to fill Nicaragua's sugar quota to the United States, seemed bleak in 1993. Restoration of the sugar quota to Nicaraguan growers has been a major blow to

Honduras's small independent producers, who had added most of Nicaragua's quota to their own during the United States embargo of Nicaragua. Higher costs for imported fertilizers because of the devaluation of the lempira add to the problem. Honduran producers seek relief from a relatively low official price of 25 lempiras per kilogram of sugar by smuggling sugar across the borders to Nicaragua and El Salvador, where the support prices are higher. Sugar growers who can afford it have begun to diversify by growing pineapples and rice. Many independent sugar growers, like independent banana producers, have become indignant over the relatively high profits shown by refiners and exporters. Strikes by producers at harvest time in 1991 forced the closure of the Choluteca refinery for a short time but had little effect on the depressed long-term outlook for the industry.

Nontraditional Crops

While the total value of export merchandise fell in 1990 and 1991 and had still not recovered in 1993 to its 1989 level, the overall agricultural sector output has grown somewhat because of growth in the sale of winter vegetables and shrimp. Nontraditional vegetables and fruit produced US$23.8 million in export revenue in 1990, a figure that was almost double the 1983 figure. Nontraditional agricultural crops represented 4.8 percent of the value of total exports in 1990, compared to 2.8 percent in 1983. Some development experts argue that government protection of corn, bean, and rice production by small farmers is a futile effort in the long-term goal of poverty reduction. On the other hand, they see significant economic potential for nontraditional crops, if they are handled properly. Analysts also note, however, that Honduras is at a distinct disadvantage relative to its Central American neighbors because of its poor transportation system. Nontraditional exports require the ability to get fresh produce from the fields to distant markets rapidly.

Livestock

In the early 1980s, the cattle industry appeared to have the potential to be an important part of the Honduran economy. The Honduran cattle sector, however, never developed to the extent that it did in much of the rest of Central America. Cattle production grew steadily until 1980-81 but then declined sharply when profits fell because of high production costs. The small Honduran meat packing industry declined at the same time, and several meat packing plants closed. As late as 1987, livestock composed 16 percent of the value-added agricultural sector but the industry continued to decline. By 1991-92, beef exports accounted for only 2.9 percent of the value of total exports.

Sales of refrigerated meat were the third or fourth highest source of export earnings in the mid-1980s, but like other Honduran agricultural products, beef yields were among the lowest in Central America. As world prices fell and production costs, exacerbated by drought, rose, there was less incentive to raise cattle. For a period of time, cattle farmers illegally smuggled beef cattle to Guatemala and other neighboring countries where prices were higher, but the Honduran cattle sector never became competitive internationally. The two large banana companies have also owned large cattle ranches where they raised prime beef, but these large companies had the flexibility to change crops as the market demanded.

Honduran dairy herds fared about the same as beef cattle, and Honduran milk yields were also among the lowest in Central America. The dairy industry was further handicapped by the difficulties of trying to transport milk over poor roads in a tropical country, as well as by stiff competition in the domestic market from subsidized foreign imports, mostly from the United States.

Fishing

Honduras significantly developed its shrimp industry during the 1980s and in the Latin American market was second only to Ecuador in shrimp exports by 1991. In 1992 shrimp and lobster jumped to 12 percent of export earnings. Shrimp contributed US$97 million in export sales to the economy in 1992 an increase of 33 percent over the previous year. The industry was dependent, however, on larvae imported from the United States to augment its unstable natural supply. Technicians from Taiwan were contracted by large producers in 1991 to help develop laboratory larvae, but bitter feuds developed between independent shrimpers and the corporations. Local shrimpers charged that corporate methods were damaging the environment and destroying natural stock through destruction of the mangrove breeding swamps. Corporate shrimp farmers then began to move their operations farther inland, leaving local shrimpers to contend with diminished natural supplies on the mosquito-infested coast.

Forestry

As in much of Central America, Honduras's once abundant forest resources have been badly squandered. In 1964 forests covered 6.8 million hectares, but by 1988 forested areas had declined to 5 million hectares. Honduras continued to lose about 3.6 percent of its remaining forests annually during the 1980s and early 1990s. The loss is attributable to several factors. Squatters have consistently used land suitable only for forests to grow scantyield food crops; large tracts have been cleared for cattle ranches; and the country has gravely mismanaged its timber resources, focusing far more effort on logging than on forestry management.

The government began an intensive forestry development program in 1974, supposedly intended to increase management of the sector and to prevent exploitation by foreign-owned firms. The Honduran Corporation for Forestry Development (Corporación Hondureña de Desarrollo Forestal Cohdefor) was created in 1974, but it quickly developed into a corrupt monopoly for overseeing forest exports. Timber was mostly produced by private sawmills under contracts selectively granted by Cohdefor officials. In fact, ongoing wasteful practices and an unsustainable debt, which was contracted to build infrastructure, appear to have undercut most conservation efforts. The military-dominated governments contracted huge debt with the multilateral development agencies, then extracted timber to pay for it. Cohdefor generally granted licenses to private lumber companies with few demands for preservation, and it had little inclination or incentive to enforce the demands it did make.

With encouragement from the United States Agency for International Development (AID), the Honduran government began to decentralize Cohdefor beginning in 1985. Under the decentralization plan, regulatory responsibilities were transferred from the central government to mayors and other municipal officials on the assumption that local officials would provide better oversight. Despite decentralization and the sale of government assets, Cohdefor's remaining debt was US$240 million in 1991. The government also assumed continued financial responsibility for the construction of a new airstrip in the area of timber extraction, upgrading facilities at Puerto Castilla and Puerto Lempira, and providing electricity at reduced prices to lumber concerns as part of the privatization package.

Major legislation was passed in 1992 to promote Honduran reforestation by making large tracts of state-owned land more accessible to private investors. The legislation also supplied subsidies for development of the sector. The same law provided for replanting mountainous regions of the country with pine to be used for fuel.

Natural Resources and Energy

Mining and Minerals

Mining, the mainstay of the Honduran economy in the late 1800s, declined dramatically in importance in the 1900s. The New York and Honduras Rosario Mining Company (NYHRMC) produced US$60 million worth of gold and silver between 1882 and 1954 before discontinuing most of its operations. Mining's contribution to the GDP steadily declined during the 1980s, to account for only a 2 percent contribution in 1992. El Mochito mine in western Honduras, the largest mine in Central America, accounted for most mineral production. Ores containing gold, silver, lead, zinc, and cadmium were mined and exported to the United States and Europe for refining.

Energy Sources

Honduras has for many years relied on fuelwood and biomass (mostly waste products from agricultural production) to supply its energy needs. The country has never been a producer of petroleum and depends on imported oil to fill much of its energy needs. In 1991 Honduras consumed about 16,000 barrels of oil daily. Honduras spent approximately US$143 million, or 13 percent of its total export earnings, to purchase oil in 1991. The country's one small refinery at Puerto Cortés closed in 1993. Various Honduran governments have done little to encourage oil exploration, although substantial oil deposits have long been suspected in the Río Sula valley and offshore along the Caribbean coast. An oil exploration consortium consisting of the Venezuelan state oil company, Venezuelan Petroleum, Inc. (Petróleos de Venezuela, S.A. PDVSA), Cambria Oil, and Texaco expressed interest in the construction of a refinery at Puerto Castilla in 1993, with production aimed at the local market.

Fuelwood and biomass have traditionally met about 67 percent of the country's total energy demand; petroleum, 29 percent; and electricity, 4 percent. In 1987 Honduran households consumed approximately 60 percent of total energy used, transportation and agriculture used about 26 percent, and industry used about 14 percent. Food processing consumed about 50 percent of industrial sector energy, followed by petroleum and chemical manufacturing.

Electric Power

Honduran electrification is low and uneven relative to other countries in Latin America. The World Bank estimates that only about 36 percent of the Honduran population had access to electricity (20 percent of the rural population) in 1987. The country's total capacity in 1992 was 575 megawatts (MW), with 2,000 megawatt-hours produced. A mammoth hydroelectric plant, the 292-MW project at El Cajón, began producing electricity in 1985 to help address the country's energy needs. The plant, however, soon became heavily indebted because of the government's electricity pricing policies (not charging public-sector institutions, for example) and because of the appointment of political cronies as top management officials. El Cajón also developed costly structural problems requiring extensive maintenance and repairs. Officials estimated that the government's decision to provide free service to publicsector institutions contributed to a 23 percent increase in publicsector consumption in 1990. Experts estimated that additional electrical generation capacity would likely be needed to keep pace with demand. The Honduran Congress assumed authority for setting electric prices beginning in 1986 but then became reluctant to increase rates. Under pressure from the World Bank, it did agree to a 60 percent increase in 1990, with additional increases in 1991. To offset these increased rates for residential users, the National Congress initiated a system of direct subsidies that ran through 1992.

Industry

Manufacturing

The country's manufacturing sector was small, contributing only 15 percent to the total GDP in 1992. Textile exports, primarily to the United States, led the Honduran manufacturing sector. The *maquiladora*, or assembly industry, was a growth industry in the generally bleak economy. Asian-owned firms dominated the sector, with twenty-one South Korean-owned companies in export processing zones located in the Río Sula valley in 1991. The *maquiladoras* employed approximately 16,000 workers in 1991; another nine firms opened in 1992. Job creation, in fact, is considered to be the primary contribution of the assembly operations to the domestic economy. The export textile manufacturing industry all but wiped out small, Honduran manufacturers, and food processors, whose goods were historically aimed at the domestic market, were also adversely affected. The small Honduran firms could not begin to compete with the assembly industry for labor because of the *maquiladoras'* relatively high wage scale of close to US$4 per day. Small firms also found it increasingly difficult to meet the high cost of mostly imported inputs. Membership in the Honduran Association of Small and Medium Industry (Asociación Hondureña de Empresas Pequeñas y Medianas) declined by 70 percent by 1991, compared to pre-*maquiladora* days, foreshadowing the likely demise of most of the small shops.

Honduran domestic manufacturers also suffered from increased Central American competition resulting from a trade liberalization pact signed in May 1991 by Honduras, El Salvador, and Guatemala. Overall, the Honduran manufacturing sector has mimicked other sectors of the economy it is mostly noncompetitive, even in a regional context, because of insufficient credit and the high cost of inputs. Relatively high interest rates and a complicated investment law have also inhibited the foreign-dominated manufacturing sector from taking off.

The government-sponsored Puerto Cortés Free Zone was opened in 1976. By 1990 an additional five free zones were in operation in Omoa, Coloma, Tela, La Ceiba, and Amapala. A series of privately run export processing zones were also established in competition with the government-sponsored free zones. These privately run zones offered the same standard import-export incentives as the government zones. Most of the government and privately run zones were located along the Caribbean coast in a newly developing industrial belt.

Firms operating outside of the special "enterprise zones" (either privately run, export-processing zones or governmentsponsored free zones) enjoy many of the same benefits as those operating within the zones. The Honduran Temporary Import Law permits companies that export 100 percent of their production to countries outside the CACM countries to hold ten-year exemptions on corporate income taxes and duty-free import of industrial inputs.

Analysts continue to debate the actual benefits of the shift away from the import-substitution industrialization (ISI) policies of the 1960s and 1970s toward a new focus on free zones and assembly industries in the 1990s. Critics point to the apparent lack of commitment by foreign manufactures to any one country site or to the creation of permanent infrastructure and employment. They question whether new employment will be enough to offset the loss of jobs in the more traditional manufacturing sector. A value of US$195 million to the Honduran economy from assembly industries in 1991 when the value of clothing exports was greater than that of coffee was a compelling argument in favor of the shift, however.

Construction

High interests rates, particularly for housing, continued to hurt the Honduran construction industry in 1993, but danger from high rates was partially offset by some public-sector investment. Privatization of formerly state-owned industries through debt swaps also negatively affected construction as prices for basic materials such as cement increased and credit tightened. A major devaluation of the lempira added to the already high cost of construction imports. Construction contributed 6.0 percent to the GDP in 1992.

Banking

The Honduran financial sector is small in comparison to the banking systems of its neighbors. After 1985, however, the sector began to grow rapidly. The average annual growth rate of value added to the economy from the financial sector for the 1980s was the second-highest in Latin America, averaging 4 percent. By 1985 Honduras had twenty-five financial institutions with 300 branch offices. Honduran commercial banks held 60 percent of the financial system's assets in 1985 and nearly 75 percent of all deposits. With the exception of the Armed Forces Social Security Institute, all commercial banks were privately owned, and most were owned by Honduran families. In 1985 there were two government-owned development banks in Honduras, one specializing in agricultural credit and the other providing financing to municipal governments.

At the behest of the International Monetary Fund (IMF) and World Bank, Honduras began a process of financial liberalization in 1990. The process began with the freeing of agricultural loan rates and was quickly followed by the freeing of loan rates in other sectors. Beginning in late 1991, Honduran banks were allowed to charge market rates for agricultural loans if they were using their own funds. By law, the banks had to report their rates to monetary authorities and could fix rates within two points of the announced rate.

In 1991 commercial banks pressured the government to reduce their 35 percent minimum reserve ratio. This rate remained standard until June 1993 when the minimum requirement was temporarily lifted to 42 percent. The rate was dropped to 36 percent three months later. The banks had excess reserves, and lending rates were in the area of 26 to 29 percent, with few borrowers. Prior to liberalization measures, the Central Bank of Honduras (Banco Central de Honduras) maintained interest rate controls, setting a 19 percent ceiling, with the market lending rate hovering around 26 percent in late 1991. With inflation hitting 33 percent in 1990, there was, in fact, a negative real interest rate, but this situation reversed in 1991 when rates were high relative to inflation. Rates of 35 to 43 percent in 1993 were well above the inflation rate of 13 to 14 percent. Bankers argued for further liberalization, including easing of controls in the housing and nonexport agricultural sectors.

A Honduran stock exchange was established in August 1990 with transactions confined to trading debt. Nine companies were registered with the exchange in 1991; in 1993 this number had grown to eighteen. It appears doubtful, however, that the market will develop fully, given the reluctance of family-held firms to open their books to public scrutiny.

Tourism

Foreign tourists are attracted to Honduras by the Mayan ruins in Cobán and coral reef skindiving off the Islas de la Bahía (Bay Islands). Poor infrastructure, however, has discouraged the development of substantial international tourism. Despite these problems, the number of visitors arriving in Honduras rose from fewer than 200,000 in 1987 to almost 250,000 in 1989. Small ecotourism projects in particular are considered to have significant potential.

Trade

In the early 1990s, the United States was by far Honduras's leading trading partner, with Japan a distant second. United States exports to Honduras in 1992 were valued at US$533 million, about 54 percent of the country's total imports of US$983 million. Most of the rest of Honduras's imports come from its Central American neighbors. Despite its status as beneficiary of both the Caribbean Basin Initiative (CBI) and the Generalized System of Preferences (GSP) both of which confer dutyfree status on Honduran imports to the United States Honduras has run a long-standing trade deficit with the United States. Total exports of goods and services by Honduras in 1992 were US$843 million, of which about 52 percent went to the United States. The current account deficit, however, continues to rise, from US$264 million in 1992 to an estimated US$370 million deficit in 1993.

Foreign Investment

With the exception of relatively recent, Asian-dominated investment in assembly firms along Honduras's northern coast, the country remains heavily dependent on United States-based multinational corporations for most of its investment needs in the early 1990s. Overall investment as a percentage of GDP declined dramatically during the 1980s, from about 25 percent in 1980 to a meager 15 percent in 1990. Dole Food Company and Chiquita Brands International together have invested heavily in Honduran industries as diverse as breweries and plastics, cement, soap, cans, and shoes.

As Honduras enters the 1990s, it faces challenging economic problems. The solutions relied on in the past traditional export crops, the *maquiladora* assembly industry, and 1980s' development schemes appear unlikely to provide enough new jobs for a rapidly growing population. The major economic challenge for Honduras over the next decade will be to find dependable sources of sustainable economic growth.

Politics and Governance

Honduras was once again in the middle of an election campaign to elect a president, representatives to the National Congress, and local leaders across the country in late 1993. The elections in November 1993 were the third since the military handed over power to a freely elected president in January 1982. Regular national elections, which have become almost holiday-like in their celebration, look to be institutionalized. For the majority of the twentieth century, the Honduran political system was dominated by two historic parties: the Liberal Party of Honduras (Partido Liberal de Honduras PLH) and the National Party of Honduras (Partido Nacional de Honduras PNH). In the 1980s, the PLH won the presidency in 1981 and 1985, with Roberto Suazo Córdova and José Azcona Hoyo, respectively; in 1989, the PNH won, with Rafael Leonardo Callejas Romero as president.

Since the 1950s, the Honduran military has been a potent domestic political force. From 1963 to 1971, and again from 1972 to 1982, the military effectively dominated the national government, frequently with the PNH's backing. After the nation was restored to civilian authority in the 1980s, the military remained a powerful political force, notably under the Suazo Córdova administration (1981-85). During that administration, the military permitted a US military presence in Nicaragua and hosted members of the Nicaraguan Resistance (more colloquially known as the Contras, short for contrarevolucionarios Spanish for counterrevolutionaries; see Glossary), a group attempting to overthrow the Nicaraguan government. The Honduran military continued to function autonomously in the early 1990s, with increased engagement in commercial enterprises.

The executive branch of government has generally dominated the legislative and judicial branches of government within the civilian government. The Honduran judiciary has been heavily chastised for partisanship and the presence of untrained judges among subordinate court officials. For the most part, the legal system has not held military or civilian elites responsible for their acts. The July 1993 conviction of two military officers for the 1991 murder of an eighteen-year-old high school student, Riccy Mabel Martnez, marked a noteworthy break from this pattern. The case aroused public opinion in Honduras against the military's protection from prosecution. The political system is likewise plagued by pervasive corruption among its ranks; bribery is an almost institutionalized practice.

A plethora of interest groups impacted the Honduran political process in the early 1990s. Despite the nation's political heritage of a strong executive branch, an intricate network of interest groups and political organizations has developed and, at times, assisted in dispute resolution. Honduras' labor movement has always been one of the most powerful in Central America. In the early 1960s and 1970s, the nation's organized peasant movement aided in the implementation of modest agricultural reform. Nonetheless, some opponents argue that the government aggressively engaged in the activities of labor unions and peasant groups in the early 1990s, particularly via the formation of "parallel unions," government-sponsored unions with minimal worker support. Honduras had a number of special interest organizations and associations active in the 1980s and 1990s, including student and women's groups, human rights organizations, and environmental organisations.

In terms of foreign policy, Honduras was emerging from a decade of regional turmoil defined by civil wars in neighboring El Salvador and Nicaragua in the early 1990s. Honduras has become a pivotal point in US strategy toward Central America in the 1980s. It housed a US-backed anti-Sandinista Contra army as well as a US military presence of 1,100 troops at Palmerola Air Base (renamed the Enrique Cano Soto Air Base in 1988). Thousands of US soldiers and National Guardsmen participated in military exercises in the nation, many of which included road construction projects, and

Honduras received over US$1.6 billion in US aid throughout the decade. However, with the conclusion of the Contra war in Nicaragua and a peace treaty in El Salvador in the early 1990s, Honduras' ties with the US shifted dramatically. Aid levels plummeted, and military aid dwindled to a trickle. The US grew increasingly prepared to criticize Honduras for its human rights record and encouraged Honduras to reduce military expenditures. However, the United States remained Honduras' most significant commercial partner and source of foreign investment, as it had in the past.

During the early 1990s, as the region's civil war was winding down, Honduras and the other Central American countries focused their efforts on regional integration, notably economic integration. The Central American presidents signed the Central American Economic Action Plan (Plan de Acción Económica de Centroamérica Paeca) in 1990, which contained promises and recommendations for economic unification. They founded the Central American Integration System (Sistema de Integración Centroamericana Sica) in 1993 as a governing organization for regional integration. The Central American Parliament (Parlamento Centroamericano Parlacen) was established in 1991 as a first step toward political unification; but, as of 1993, only Honduras, Guatemala, and El Salvador, the so-called northern triangle governments, have elected members to that body. Honduras' long-running border issue with El Salvador was concluded in September 1992, when the International Court of Justice (ICJ) gave Honduras about two-thirds of the disputed area. Both countries decided to accept the verdict, which many saw as a triumph for Honduras.

The Constitution

The Honduran constitution, the sixteenth since independence from Spain, entered into force on January 20, 1982. Just a week before, Honduras had ended ten years of military rule with the inauguration of civilian president Roberto Suazo Córdova. The constitution was completed on January 11, 1982, by a seventy-one-seat Constituent Assembly that had been elected on April 20, 1980, under the military junta of Policarpo Paz García. The Constituent Assembly was dominated by Honduras's two major political parties, the PLH, which held thirty-five seats, and the PNH, which held thirty-three seats. The small Innovation and Unity Party (Partido de Inovación y Unidad Pinu) held the remaining three seats.

Honduran constitutions are generally held to have little bearing on Honduran political reality because they are considered aspirations or ideals rather than legal instruments of a working government. The constitution essentially provides for the separation of powers among the three branches of government, but in practice the executive branch generally dominates both the legislative and judicial branches of government. Moreover, according to the United States Department of State's human rights report for 1992, although basic human rights are protected in the constitution, in practice the government has been unable to assure that many violations are fully investigated, or that most of the perpetrators, either military or civilian, are brought to justice.

Of the nation's fifteen previous constitutions, several have marked significant milestones in the nation's political development. The first constitution, in 1825, which reflected strong Spanish influence, established three branches of government. The 1839 constitution, which emphasized the protection of individual rights, was the nation's first outside the framework of the United Provinces of Central America; Honduras had just declared independence from the federation in October 1838. In the 1865 constitution, the right of habeas corpus was constitutionally guaranteed for the first time. The 1880 constitution introduced many new features to the Honduran political system, including the principle of municipal autonomy and the state's role in promoting economic development. Separation of church and state was also an important feature, as previous constitutions had proclaimed Roman Catholicism as the state's official religion.

Promulgated under the presidency of Policarpo Bonilla Vásquez (1894-99), the 1894 constitution the nation's ninth was considered the most progressive in its time. It abolished the death penalty and elevated the status of laws covering the press, elections, and *amparo*, laws that granted protection to claims in litigation. Although many provisions of the 1894 constitution were ignored, the document served as a model for future constitutions. The 1924 constitution introduced new social and labor provisions and attempted to make the legislature a stronger institution vis-à-vis the executive branch. With the 1936 constitution, which was promulgated under the dictatorship of Tiburcio Carías Andino (1933-49), the powers of the executive were again reinforced, and the presidential and legislative terms of office were extended from four to six years. Some observers maintain that the 1936 constitution was amended on numerous occasions to serve the needs of the Cariato, as the dictatorship came to be known.

The 1957 constitution, promulgated under the presidency of Ramón Villeda Morales (1958-63), introduced a number of new features, including labor provisions (influenced by the growth of trade unionism after the banana strike of 1954) and the establishment of a body to regulate the electoral process. The 1965 constitution, the nation's fifteenth, was promulgated under the military rule of Colonel Osvaldo López Arellano (1963-71, 1972-73) and remained in force until 1982, through the brief civilian presidency of Ramón Ernesto Cruz (1971-72) and through ten more years of military rule.

The 1982 constitution provides for many of the governmental institutions and processes inherited from previous decades. Throughout the constitution, however, new or changed provisions help distinguish it from previous constitutions, and some analysts consider it the most advanced constitution in Honduran history. The preamble expresses faith in the restoration of the Central American union and emphasizes the rule of law as a means of achieving a just society.

The 1982 constitution consists of a preamble and 379 articles divided into eight titles that are further divided into forty-three chapters. The first seven titles cover substantive provisions delineating the rights of individuals and the organization and responsibilities of the Honduran state. The last title provides for the constitution's implementation and amendment. As of mid-1993, the National Congress had amended the 1982 constitution on seven occasions and interpreted specific provisions of the constitution on four occasions.

The organization of the Honduran state, national territory, and international treaties are covered in Title I of the constitution. As stated in Article 4, "The government is republican, democratic and representative" and "composed of three branches: legislative, executive and judicial, which are complementary, independent, and not subordinate to each other." In practice, however, the executive branch has dominated the other two branches of government. Article 2, which states that sovereignty originates in the people, also includes a provision new to the 1982 constitution that labels the supplanting of popular sovereignty and the usurping of power as "crimes of treason against the fatherland." This provision can be considered an added constitutional protection of representative democracy in a country in which the military has a history of usurping power from elected civilian governments.

Title II addresses nationality and citizenship, suffrage and political parties, and provides for an independent and autonomous National Elections Tribunal (Tribunal Nacional de Elecciones TNE) to handle all matters relating to electoral acts and procedures. Provisions regarding nationality and citizenship are essentially the same as in the 1965 constitution, with one significant exception. In the 1965 document, Central Americans by birth were considered "native-born Hondurans" after one year of residence in Honduras and after completing certain legal procedures, but in the 1982 constitution (Article 24), Central Americans by birth who have resided in the country for one year are Hondurans by naturalization. With regard to the electoral system, Article 46 provides for election through proportional or majority representation.

Individual rights and guarantees for Honduras citizens are addressed in Title III. This section covers such matters as social, child, and labor rights; social security; and health, education, culture, and housing issues. Different from the 1965 constitution is the chapter devoted entirely to "rights of the child."

The rights of habeas corpus and *amparo* are provided for in Title IV, which also addresses the constitutional review of laws by the Supreme Court of Justice and cases when constitutional guarantees may be restricted or suspended.

Title V outlines the branches and offices of the government and their responsibilities, and spells out the procedure for the enactment, sanction, and promulgation of laws. It covers the legislative, executive, and judicial branches of government; the Office of the Comptroller General and the Directorate of Administrative Probity, both of which are auxiliary but independent agencies of the legislative branch; the Office of the Attorney General, the legal representative of the Honduran state; the offices of the ministers of the cabinet, with no fewer than twelve ministries; the civil service; the departmental and municipal system of local government; and guidelines for the establishment of decentralized institutions of the Honduran state. Different from the 1965 constitution, the terms of legislators and the president are four years, instead of six years. Another new feature focuses on the development of local government throughout the country. Article 299 states that "economic and social development of the municipalities must form part of the national development program," whereas Article 302, in order to ensure the improvement and development of the municipalities, encourages citizens to form civic associations, federations, or confederations.

The chapter on the judiciary also contains several changes from the 1965 constitution. The changes, according to one analysis, appear to bring the administration of justice closer to the people. Article 303 declares that "the power to dispense justice emanates from the people and is administered free of charge on behalf of the state by independent justices and judges." The Supreme Court of Justice has nine principal justices and seven alternates, increased from the seven principals and five alternates provided in the 1965 document.

Title V also includes a chapter covering the armed forces, which consists of the "high command, army, air force, navy, public security force, and the agencies and units determined by the laws establishing them." Most provisions of this chapter are largely the same as in the 1965 and 1957 constitutions. As set forth in Article 272, the armed forces are to be an "essentially professional, apolitical, obedient, and nondeliberative national institution"; in practice, however, the Honduran military essentially has enjoyed autonomy vis-à-vis civilian authority since 1957. The president retains the title of general commander over the armed forces, as provided in Article 245 (16). Orders given by the president to the armed forces, through its commander in chief, must be obeyed and executed, as provided in Article 278. The armed forces, however, is under the direct command of the commander in chief of the armed forces (Article 277); and it is through him that the president performs his constitutional duty relating to the armed forces. According to Article 285, the Supreme Council of the Armed Forces (Consejo Superior de las Fuerzas Armadas Consuffaa) is the armed forces consultative organ. The Supreme Council is chaired by the commander in chief of the armed forces, who is elected by the National Congress for a term of three years. He is chosen from a list of three officers proposed by Consuffaa. In practice, the National Congress always approves (some observers would say rubberstamps) Consuffaa's first choice.

The nation's economic regime, covered in Title VI, "is based on the principles of efficiency in production and social justice in the distribution of wealth and national income, as well as on the harmonious coexistence of the factors of production." As provided in Article 329, the Honduran state is involved in the promotion of economic and social development, subject to appropriate planning. The title also includes provisions on currency and banking, agrarian reform (which is declared to be of public need and interest), the tax system, public wealth, and the national budget.

Title VII, with two chapters, outlines the process of amending the constitution and sets forth the principle of constitutional inviolability. The constitution may be amended by the National Congress after a two-thirds vote of all its members in two consecutive regular annual sessions. However, several constitutional provisions may not be amended. These consist of the amendment process itself, as well as provisions covering the form of government, national territory, and several articles covering the presidency, including term of office and prohibition from reelection.

Governmental Institutions and Process

Executive

The executive branch in Honduras, headed by a president who is elected by a simple majority, has traditionally dominated the legislative and judicial branches of government. According to political scientist Mark B. Rosenberg, the entire Honduran government apparatus is dependent on the president, who defines or structures policy (with the exception of security policy, which remains in the military's realm) through legislation or policy decrees. However, Rosenberg also notes that in an environment of intense rivalry and animosity between the two major parties, in which the president is under pressure to reward his party's supporters, public policy initiatives often do not fare well, as the executive becomes bogged down with satisfying more pressing parochial needs.

Political scientist James Morris points out that the executive-centered nature of the Honduran political system has endured whether the head of state has been an elected civilian politician or a general, and that the Honduran state's formal and informal center of authority is the executive.

According to the constitution, the president has responsibility for drawing up a national development plan, discussing it in the cabinet, submitting it to the National Congress for approval, directing it, and executing it. He or she directs the economic and financial policy of the state, including the supervision and control of banking institutions, insurance companies, and investment houses through the National Banking and Insurance Commission. The president has responsibility for prescribing feasible measures to promote the rapid execution of agrarian reform and the development of production and productivity in rural areas. With regard to education policy, the president is responsible for organizing, directing, and promoting education as well as for eradicating illiteracy and improving technical education. With regard to health policy, the president is charged with adopting measures for the promotion, recovery, and rehabilitation of the population's health, as well as for disease prevention. The president also has responsibility for directing and supporting economic and social integration, both national and international, aimed at improving living conditions for Hondurans. In addition, the president directs foreign policy and relations, and may conclude treaties and agreements with foreign nations. He or she appoints the heads of diplomatic and consular missions.

With regard to the legislative branch, the president participates in the enactment of laws by introducing bills in the National Congress through the cabinet ministers. The president has the power to sanction, veto, or promulgate and publish any laws approved by the National Congress. The president may convene the National Congress into special session, through a Permanent Committee of the National Congress, or may propose the continuation of the regular annual session. The president may send messages to the National Congress at any time and must deliver an annual message to the National Congress in person at the beginning of each regular legislative session. In addition, although the constitution gives the National Congress the power to elect numerous government officials (such as Supreme Court justices, the comptroller general, the attorney general, and the director of administrative probity), these selections are essentially made by the president and rubberstamped by the National Congress.

The constitution sets forth forty-five powers of the National Congress, the most important being the power to make, enact, interpret, and repeal laws. Legislative bills may be introduced in the National Congress by any deputy or the president (through the cabinet ministers). The Supreme Court of Justice and the TNE may also introduce bills within their jurisdiction. In practice, most legislation and policy initiatives are introduced by the executive branch, although there are some instances where legislation and initiatives emanate from the National Congress. A bill must be debated on three different days before being voted upon, with the exception of urgent cases as determined by a simple majority of the deputies present. If approved, the measure is sent to the executive branch for sanction and promulgation. In general, a law is considered compulsory after promulgation and after twenty days from being published in the official journal, *Gaceta Judicial*. If the president does not veto the bill within ten days, it is considered sanctioned and is to be promulgated by the president.

If the president vetoes a measure, he must return it to the National Congress within ten days explaining the grounds for disapproval. To approve the bill again, the National Congress must again debate it and then ratify it by a two-thirds majority vote, whereupon it is sent to the executive branch for immediate publication. However, if the president originally vetoed the bill on the grounds that it was unconstitutional, the bill cannot be debated in the National Congress until the Supreme Court renders its opinion on the measure within a timeframe specified by the National Congress. If an executive veto is not overridden by the National Congress, the bill may not be debated again in the same session of the National Congress.

If the National Congress approves a bill at the end of its session, and the president intends to veto it, the president must immediately notify the National Congress so that it can extend the session for ten days beyond when it receives the disapproved bill. If the president does not comply with this procedure, he must return the bill within the first eight days of the next session of the National Congress.

Certain acts and resolutions of the National Congress may not be vetoed by the president. Most significantly these include the budget law, amendments to the constitution, declarations regarding grounds for impeachment for high-ranking government officials, and decrees relating to the conduct of the executive branch.

With regard to security, the president is charged with maintaining peace and internal security of the nation and with repelling every attack or external aggressor. During a recess of the National Congress, the president may declare war and make peace, although the National Congress must be convened immediately. The president may restrict or suspend certain individual rights and guarantees with the concurrence of the cabinet for a period of forty-five days, a period that may be renewed. (Article 187 of the constitution spells out the procedure to be followed for the suspension of rights.) The president may deny or permit, after congressional authorization, the transit of foreign troops through Honduran territory. The president is also charged with monitoring the official behavior of public officials for the security and prestige of the Honduran government and state.

In theory, the president exercises command over the armed forces as the general commander and adopts necessary measures for the defense of the nation. The president confers military ranks for second lieutenant through captain based on the proposal of the commander in chief of the armed forces. Most importantly, the president is charged with ensuring that the army is apolitical, essentially professional, and obedient. In practice, however, the military operates autonomously. According to the view of Honduran political scientist Ernesto Paz Aguilar, the armed forces is the country's principal political force, exercising a tutelary role over the other institutions of government and constituting a de facto power that is not subordinate to civilian political power. Other observers, although acknowledging the military is a politically powerful institution, maintain that the military essentially confines its spheres of influence to national security and internal stability, although in recent years, they concede that the military has had an increasing role in economic activities.

Serving under the president are the ministers of the cabinet, who cooperate with the president in coordinating, directing, and supervising the organs and agencies of the executive branch under their jurisdiction. As required by Article 246 of the constitution, there are to be at least twelve departments of the cabinet covering the following portfolios: government and justice; the Office of the President; foreign affairs; economy and commerce; finance and public credit; national defense and public security; labor and social welfare; public health and social aid; public education; communications, public works, and transport; culture and tourism; and natural resources. In addition to these ministries, in the early 1990s, there was also another cabinet-level department, the Ministry of Planning, Coordination, and Budget. The National Congress may summon the cabinet ministers to answer questions relating to their portfolios. Within the first days of the installation of the National Congress, ministers must submit annually a report on the work done in their respective ministries. The president convokes and presides over the cabinet ministers in a body known as the Council of Ministers, which, according to the constitution, meets at the president's initiative to make decisions on any matters he or she considers of national importance and to consider such cases specified by law.

In addition to the various ministries, the president may create commissions, either permanent or temporary, made up of public officials or other representatives of Honduran sectors to undertake certain projects or programs mandated by the executive. The president may also name commissioners to coordinate the action of public entities and agencies of the state or to develop programs.

The Callejas (1990-) government created several presidential commissions for certain projects or programs. In 1990 Callejas established and headed the Modernization of the State Commission, which included thirty representatives of governmental institutions, the four legally recognized political parties, business, and labor. The objective of the commission was to study and design national policies for reforming the functioning of the Honduran state, including reform of the legislature and judiciary, decentralization of the power of the executive branch in favor of the municipalities, and modernizing public administration.

In December 1992, the Callejas government appointed a head to the National Commission for the Protection of Human Rights (Comisión Nacional para la Protección de Derechos Humanos Conaprodeh), a new position established to protect the rights of persons who consider themselves victims of abuse or an unjust act by judicial or public administration.

In 1993 the Callejas government established two additional commissions, a Fiscal Intervention Commission to investigate governmental corruption that began with an inquiry into corruption at the Customs Directorate, and a high-level ad hoc Commission for Institutional Reform, headed by Roman Catholic Archbishop Oscar Andrés Rodríguez. The ad hoc commission, created in early March 1993, was established to formulate recommendations within thirty days for specific measures to improve the security forces, especially the National Directorate of Investigations (Directorio de

Investigación Nacional DIN), and to strengthen the judiciary and public prosecutor's office. The DNI was created because of growing public criticism of the DNI and military impunity. It had representatives from each branch of government, from the military, from each of the four 1993 presidential candidates, and from the mass media.

The Honduran civil service system regulates employment in the public sector, theoretically based on the principles of competence, efficiency, and honesty, according to the constitution. In practice, however, the system has been a source of political patronage, which some observers claim has led to a bloated bureaucracy. In 1990 there were an estimated 70,000 government employees, including employees of the decentralized institutions. Economic austerity measures introduced by the Callejas government reportedly led to the dismissal of thousands of employees, although some claim that thousands of other employees were hired because of political patronage. According to some observers, a fundamental problem of the Honduran civil service is its politicization, whereby much of the bureaucracy is replaced when the ruling party changes. Traditionally, in Honduras, political patronage has been a key characteristic of the two dominant political parties. According to political scientist Mark B. Rosenberg, a president once in office is under tremendous pressure to provide jobs, recommendations, and other rewards to his followers in exchange for their continued loyalty and support.

In addition to the various ministries, there are also numerous autonomous and semiautonomous state entities within the executive branch, which have increased in number over the years as the government has become more involved in the economic development process and the provision of basic services. These decentralized institutions vary in their composition, structure, and function, but include three basic types: public institutes, which are largely government-funded and perform social or collective services that are not usually provided by the private sector; public enterprises, which often have their own resource bases and are autonomous organs of the state; and mixed enterprises, which bring together the government and private sector, with the state retaining at least a 51 percent share of the enterprise. Among the best known decentralized agencies in Honduras are the National Autonomous University of Honduras (Universidad Nacional Autónoma de Honduras UNAH); the Central Bank of Honduras (Banco Central de Honduras); the National Agrarian Institute (Instituto Nacional Agrario INA); the Honduran Banana Corporation (Corporación Hondureña de Bananas); the Honduran Forestry Development Corporation (Corporación Hondureña de Desarrollo Forestal Cohdefor); the Honduran Coffee Institute (Corporación Hondureña deCafe); the Honduran Social Security Institute (Instituto Hondureño de Seguro Social IHSS); the National Council of Social Welfare (Consejo Nacional de Bienestar Social); and the National Electric Energy Enterprise (Empresa Nacional de Energía Eléctrica).

Legislative

The legislative branch consists of the unicameral National Congress elected for a four-year term of office at the same time as the president. When the country returned to civilian democratic rule in 1982, the National Congress had a membership of eighty-two deputies. This number was increased to 134 deputies for the 1985 national elections and then reduced to 128 for the 1989 national elections it remained 128 for the 1993 national elections. The constitution, as amended in 1988, establishes a fixed number of 128 principal deputies and the same number of alternate deputies. If the principal deputy cannot complete his or her term, the National Congress may call the alternate deputy to serve the remainder of the term.

The National Congress conducts regular annual sessions beginning on January 25 and adjourning on October 31. These sessions, however, may be extended. In addition, special sessions may be called at the request of the executive branch through the Permanent Committee of Congress, provided that a simple majority of deputies agrees. A simple majority of the total number of principal deputies also constitutes a quorum for the installation of the National Congress and the holding of meetings. The Permanent Committee of Congress is a body of nine deputies and their alternates, appointed before the end of regular sessions, that remains on duty during the adjournment of the National Congress. The National Congress is headed by a directorate that is elected by a majority of deputies, which is headed by a president (who also presides over the Permanent Committee of Congress when the National Congress is not in session) and includes at least two vice presidents and two ministers.

In fulfilling its responsibilities, the National Congress has numerous commissions or committees for the study of issues that come before the legislature. In addition to committees that cover legislation (first, second, and third debate), protocol, and the budget, many other committees parallel the ministries of the executive branch, including government and justice, foreign affairs, economic affairs and trade, finance and public credit, national defense and security, public health, public education, communications and public works, labor and social welfare, natural resources, and culture and tourism. According to the internal regulations of the National Congress, between three and seven deputies sit on each committee. In addition, nonstanding or extraordinary committees may cover other issues, and special committees may be established to investigate matters of national interest. Because of the executive-driven nature of the legislative process, the committees are somewhat underutilized and play only a minor role in the legislative process or congressional decision making. Aggravating this underutilization is the fact that no staff members are assigned to the committees, so that necessary studies or reports for the committees must be are solicited from outside of the National Congress.

In addition to its legislative activities, the National Congress also has other extensive powers, particularly regarding other branches of the government and other institutions of the Honduran state. The National Congress is charged with electing numerous government officials: the nine principal justices and seven alternates of the Supreme Court of Justice, including its president; the commander in chief of the armed forces; the comptroller general; the attorney general; and the director of administrative probity. In practice, however, the National Congress generally rubberstamps the choices of the president, or, in the case of the commander in chief of the armed forces, of the military. The National Congress may declare that there are grounds for impeachment of certain high-ranking government officials, including the president and presidential designates, Supreme Court justices, cabinet ministers and deputy secretaries, and the commander in chief of the armed forces.

In its oversight role, the National Congress may approve or disapprove the administrative conduct of the other two branches of government, the TNE, the comptroller general, the attorney general, and the decentralized institutions. The National Congress may also question the cabinet secretaries and other officials of the government, decentralized institutions, and other entities concerning matters related to public administration.

With regard to the military and national security, as noted above, the National Congress elects the commander in chief of the armed forces from a list of three proposed by the Consuffaa. The National Congress may fix the permanent number of members of the armed forces and confer all ranks from major to major general, at the joint proposal of the commander in chief of the armed forces and the president. It may authorize or refuse the president's request for the crossing of foreign troops through national territory. It may also authorize the entrance of foreign military missions of technical assistance or cooperation in the country. The National Congress may declare an executive-branch restriction or suspension of individual rights or guarantees in accordance with constitutional provisions, or it may modify or disapprove of the restriction or suspension enacted by the president.

With regard to foreign policy, the National Congress has the power to declare war or make peace at the request of the president. The National Congress also may approve or disapprove international treaties signed by the executive branch.

Regarding government finances, the National Congress is charged with adopting annually (and modifying if desired) the general budget of revenue and expenditures based on the executive branch's proposal. The National Congress has control over public revenues and has power to levy taxes, assessments, and other public charges. It approves or disapproves the formal accounts of public expenditures based on reports submitted by the comptroller general and loans and similar agreements related to public credit entered into by the executive branch.

The legislative branch has two auxiliary agencies, the Office of the Comptroller General and the Directorate of Administrative Probity, both of which are functionally and administratively independent. The Office of the Comptroller General is exclusively responsible for the post-auditing of the public treasury. It maintains the administration of public funds and properties and audits the accounts of officials and employees who handle these funds and properties. It audits the financial operations of agencies, entities, and institutions of the government, including decentralized institutions. It examines the books kept by the state and accounts rendered by the executive branch to the National Congress on the operations of the public treasury and reports to the National Congress on its findings. The Directorate of Administrative Probity audits the accounts of public officials or employees to prevent their unlawful enrichment.

Some observers maintain that the National Congress gradually became a more effective and independent institution in the decade after the country returned to civilian rule in 1982. According to political scientist Mark Rosenberg, under the presidency of Suazo

Córdova the institution appeared only to function as a rubber stamp for the executive branch, with little interest in promoting or creating policy initiatives. Under the Azcona government (1986-90), however, the National Congress became more assertive in its relations with the executive branch with a more vigorous use of its oversight powers and more active interest in developing legislation. This trend continued under the Callejas presidency. In 1993 a new legislative support body, the Data Processing and Legislative Studies Center (Centro de Informática y Estudios Legislativas CIEL), was created with the assistance of the United States Agency for International Development (AID) to help provide computer and analytical support to the committees and deputies of the National Congress.

Other observers stress the executive dominance over the legislative branch in almost all areas of public policy. They point out that the tradition of a strong executive is deeply embedded in the national psyche, with the National Congress itself not willing or able to take responsibility for its congressional obligations. The general public view of the National Congress is that deputies use their offices for personal and political gain. As a result, most people contact executive branch officials to promote causes, a practice that reinforces executive dominance and makes it difficult for the congressional leadership to transform the National Congress into an equal partner in government.

The nation's electoral law also limits the independence and ultimately the effectiveness of the National Congress. Elections for the National Congress are held at the same time as presidential elections, and voters must use a unitary ballot that contains a party's presidential candidate, as well as its list of congressional candidates for each department. Voters are not allowed to split their tickets for national offices; however, in November 1993, voters for the first time could spilt their ticket for president and mayor. The percentage of votes that a presidential candidate receives in each department determines the number of deputies from each party selected to represent that department. In effect, voters are not sure whom they are electing to the National Congress. There is no direct accountability to the electorate. Instead, deputies respond to party leadership, and party loyalty and bloc voting are the norm. The two major parties dominate the National Congress, with smaller parties finding it difficult to gain representation. In the 1989 national elections, the PNH won seventy-one seats in the National Congress, and the PLH captured fifty-five seats. The small Pinu won just two seats, and the Honduran Christian Democratic Party (Partido Demócrata Cristiano de Honduras PDCH) gained no seats. Efforts to change the unitary ballot for the presidential and legislative candidates for the November 1993 elections were unsuccessful, largely because the two dominant parties overcame pressure by the two smaller parties for separate ballots.

Judiciary

The judicial branch of government consists of a Supreme Court of Justice, courts of appeal, courts of first instance (Juzgados de Letras), and justices of the peace. The Supreme Court, which is the court of last resort, has nine principal justices and seven alternates. The Supreme Court has fourteen constitutional powers and duties. These include the appointment of judges and justices of the lower courts and public prosecutors; the power to declare laws to be unconstitutional; the power to try high-ranking government officials when the National Congress has declared that there are grounds for impeachment; and publication of the court's official record, the *Gaceta Judicial*. The court has three chambers civil, criminal, and labor with three justices assigned to each chamber.

Organizationally below the Supreme Court are the courts of appeal. These courts are three-judge panels that hear all appeals from the lower courts, including civil, commercial, criminal and habeas corpus cases. To be eligible to sit on these courts, the judges must be attorneys and at least twenty-five years old. In the early 1990s, there were nine courts of appeal, four in Tegucigalpa, two in San Pedro Sula, and one each in La Ceiba, Comayagua, and Santa Bárbara. Two of these courts of appeal, one in the capital and one in San Pedro Sula, specialized in labor cases. In addition, a contentious-administrative court, which dealt with public administration, was located in Tegucigalpa, but had jurisdiction throughout the country.

The next level of courts are first instance courts, which serve as trial courts in serious civil and criminal cases. In the early 1990s, there were sixty-four such courts. Although half of the first instance courts were in Tegucigalpa and San Pedro Sula, each departmental capital had at least one. Half of the sixty-four courts covered both civil and criminal cases, eight just covered criminal cases, and seven covered civil cases. There were also six labor courts, six family courts, two juvenile courts, two tenant courts, and one contentious-administrative court. Most of the judges, who must be at least twenty-one years old, held degrees in juridical science. Although judges are required to be licensed attorneys, many in fact are not.

The lowest level of the court system consists of justices of the peace distributed throughout the country. Each department capital and municipalities with populations of more than 4,000 are supposed to have two justices, and municipalities with populations less than 4,000 are supposed to have one justice of the peace. Justices of the peace handling criminal cases act as investigating magistrates and are involved only in minor cases. More serious criminal cases are handled by the first instance courts. Justices of the peace must be more than twenty-one years of age, live in the municipality where they have jurisdiction, and have the ability to read and write. In 1990 there were an estimated 320 justices of the peace, with thirty responsible for civil cases, thirty for criminal cases, and the remaining 260 justices covering both civil and criminal cases. Political patronage has traditionally been the most important factor in appointing justices of the peace, and this practice has often led to less than qualified judicial personnel, some of whom have not completed primary education.

The constitution requires that the judicial branch of government is to receive not less than 3 percent of the annual national budget, but in practice this requirement has never been met. For example, in 1989 the judiciary received 1.63 percent of the national budget, just slightly more than one-half of the amount constitutionally required.

As in previous years, in the early 1990s the Honduran judicial system has been the subject of numerous criticisms, including widespread corruption and continuing ineffectiveness with regard to holding military members or civilian elites accountable for their crimes. According to the United States Department of State's human rights report for 1992, the civilian judiciary in Honduras "is weak, underfunded, politicized, inefficient, and corrupt." The report further charged that the judiciary remains vulnerable to outside influence and suffers from woefully inadequate funding, and that the Callejas government is unable to ensure that many human rights violations are fully investigated, or that most of the perpetrators, either military or civilian, are brought to justice. Justice is reported to be applied inequitably, with the poor punished according to the law, but the rich or politically influential almost never brought to trial, much less convicted or jailed.

One frequent criticism has focused on the executive branch's dominance over the judiciary. Because a new Supreme Court is appointed every four years with the change in the presidency and because the executive essentially controls the selection of the justices, the judiciary is largely beholden to the president. This loyalty to the executive permeates the judicial branch because the Supreme Court appoints all lower court justices. To eliminate this partisanship in the courts, the Modernization of the State Commission, established by President Callejas, proposed that the constitution be amended to change the way Supreme Court justices are appointed. According to the proposal, justices would hold seven-year appointments and would be selected from a list of candidates developed by a special committee composed of those who work in the justice sector.

Another criticism notes that judicial personnel are often unqualified for their positions. Although a Judicial Career Law (which requires that all hiring and promotions be based on merit and that all firings based on cause) was approved in 1980, the government did not begin implementing the law until 1991 because of the overall lack of political will. The United States Department of State's human rights report for 1992 maintained that results have been few, but AID states that the law could be fully implemented by 1995. AID has lent support to the Honduran court since 1985 and in 1989 began an experimental program designed to improve the selection process for justices of the peace so that the appointed justices would hold law degrees. By 1991 the AID program accounted for the qualifications of eighty-one justices of the peace, and AID estimated that by 1995 about half of all justices of the peace would have law degrees.

Closely associated with the judicial system and the administration of justice in Honduras is the Office of the Attorney General, which, as provided in the constitution, is the legal representative of the state, representing the state's interests. Both the attorney general and the deputy attorney general are elected by the National Congress for a period of four years, coinciding with the presidential and legislative terms of office. The attorney general is expected to initiate civil and criminal actions based on the results of the audits of the Office of the Comptroller General. The law creating the Office of the Attorney General was first enacted in 1961.

Although some public prosecutors operate out of the Office of the Attorney General, most operate out of the Office of the Public Prosecutor of the Supreme Court. The public prosecutor of the Supreme Court also serves as chief of the Prosecutor General's Office (Ministerio Público) as provided under the 1906 Law of the Organization and Attributions of the Courts. In April 1993, the Ad Hoc Commission for Institutional Reform created by President

Callejas recommended the creation of a Prosecutor General's Office as an independent, autonomous, and apolitical organization, not under either the Supreme Court or the Office of the Attorney General. The prosecutor general would be appointed by the National Congress by a two-thirds vote for a seven-year appointment. The ad hoc commission also recommended that this new Prosecutor General's Office have under it a newly created Department of Criminal Investigation (Departamento de Investigación Criminal DIC), a police and investigatory corps that would replace the current DIN, a department of the Public Security Force (Fuerza de Seguridad Pública Fusep) that has often been associated with human rights abuses.

Local Government

Honduras is administratively divided into eighteen departments (Atlántida, Choluteca, Colón, Comayagua, Copán, Cortés, El Paraíso, Francisco Morazán, Gracias a Dios, Intibucá, Islas de la Bahía (Bay Islands), La Paz, Lempira, Ocotepeque, Olancho, Santa Bárbara, Valle, and Yoro), each with a designated department capital (*cabecera*). The president of the republic freely appoints, and may freely remove, governors for each department. Departmental governors represent the executive branch in official acts in their department and serve as the tie between the executive branch and other national agencies and institutions that might have delegations working in the department. Each governor may freely appoint and remove a secretary to assist him or her. If a governor is absent more than five days, the mayor of the departmental capital substitutes for the governor. The costs of running the departmental governments fall under the budget of the Ministry of Government and Justice.

The departments are further divided into 291 municipalities (*municipios*) nationwide, including a Central District consisting of the cities of Tegucigalpa and Comayagüela. A municipality in

Honduras may include more than one city within its boundaries, and is therefore similar to the jurisdiction of county in the United States. In addition to cities, municipalities may also include *aldeas* (villages) and *caseríos* (hamlets), which are scattered concentrations of populations outside urban areas. The urbanized cities may be divided into smaller divisions known as *colonias* (colonies) and barrios (neighborhoods).

The municipalities are administered by elected corporations, deliberative organs that are accountable to the courts of justice for abuses, and are supposed to be autonomous or independent of the central government's powers. The municipal corporations consist of a mayor (*alcalde*), who is the paramount executive authority in a municipality, and a municipal council that varies in size depending on the population of the municipality. Those municipalities with a population of less than 5,000 have four council members, those with a population of between 5,000 and 10,000 have six, and those with a population between 10,000 and 80,000 have eight. All the department capitals, regardless of their population, and municipalities with a population of more than 80,000 have ten council members.

The municipal corporations meet at least two times per month in ordinary sessions, but special sessions may be called by the mayor or by at least two council members. Each municipal corporation has a secretary, freely appointed and removed by a majority of the members of the corporation, and a treasurer, named by the corporation at the request of the mayor. Municipalities with annual revenue of more than one million lempiras are to have an auditor named by the municipal corporation; however, in the early 1990s, the majority of Honduran municipalities had an annual revenue of less than one million lempiras.

The constitution sets forth several provisions regarding the municipalities. According to Article 299, the economic and social development of the municipalities must form part of the nation's development plans. Each municipality is also to have sufficient communal land in order to ensure its existence and development. Citizens of municipalities are entitled to form civic associations, federations, or confederations in order to ensure the improvement and development of the municipalities. In general, income and investment taxes in a municipality are paid into the municipal treasury.

In 1990 a new Law of Municipalities covering both departmental and municipal administration superseded the previous municipal law issued in 1927. The new law set forth the numerous rights and responsibilities of the municipalities and public administration at the municipal level. It also outlined the concept of municipal autonomy, characterized by free elections; free public administration and decisions; the collection and investment of resources with special attention on the preservation of the environment; the development, approval, and administration of a municipal budget; the organization and management of public services; the right of the municipality to create its own administrative structure; and municipal control over natural resources. The law also outlines twenty-one functions of the municipal corporations, which include the following responsibilities: organizing public administration and services, developing and implementing a municipal budget, appointing public employees and naming needed public commissions, planning urban development, and consulting the public through plebiscites on important municipal issues and through open public meetings with representatives of the various social sectors of the municipality.

Under the law, each municipality has a Municipal Development Council named by the corporation and consisting of representatives of the various economic and social sectors of the municipality. The Municipal Development Council functions in an advisory capacity by providing the corporations with information and input for making decisions. The law also calls for a special law to be enacted to regulate the organization and functioning of a national Institute of Municipal Development to promote the integrated development of municipalities in Honduras.

Traditionally, the central government in Honduras, whether civilian or military, has dominated local government, and some observers maintain that local mayors and municipal corporations have served largely as administrative arms of the central government. With the return to democratic rule in 1982, however, there has been a shift, at least in theory, to promote the economic development and political independence of the municipalities. New provisions in the 1982 constitution call for economic and social development in the municipalities to form parts of national development programs and outline the right of citizens to form organizations to ensure the improvement and development of the municipalities.

The Callejas government emphasized support for political and administrative decentralization from the executive branch to the municipalities. In fact, one of the objectives in establishing the Modernization of the State Commission in 1990 was to reduce the centralism of the executive branch through the effective and orderly transfer of functions and resources to the municipalities in order to fortify their autonomy. The promulgation of the new Law of Municipalities in 1990 was further evidence of the Callejas government's emphasis on municipal development. Observers noted, however, that the executive branch, particularly through the decentralized agencies and institutions, still wielded significant power at the local level in the early 1990s.

One significant measure approved in 1992 was reform of the nation's electoral law for the 1993 national elections. For the first time, the law would allow voters to cast their ballots separately for mayoral candidates. In previous elections, the practice of split-party voting was not allowed, and the mayors were elected based on the percentage of the vote received by the presidential candidates. The reform of the electoral law is significant in that it makes elected mayors directly accountable to the electorate and strengthens the democratic process at the local level. The reform could also strengthen the chances for the nation's two smaller parties to gain representation in the municipalities.

The Electoral Process

The president is elected along with three presidential designates (who essentially function as vice presidents) for fouryear terms of office beginning on January 27. The president and the presidential designates must be Honduran by birth, more than thirty years old, and enjoy the rights of Honduran citizenship. Additional restrictions prohibit public servants and members of the military from serving as president. Commanders and general officers of the armed forces and senior officers of the police or state security forces are ineligible. Active-duty members of any armed body are not eligible if they have performed their functions during the previous twelve months before the election. The relatives (fourth degree by blood and second degree by marriage) and spouse of each military officer serving on Consuffaa are also ineligible, as are the relatives of the president and the presidential delegates. Numerous high-level public servants, including the presidential designates, cabinet secretaries and deputy secretaries, members of the TNE, and justices and judges of the judicial branch, are prohibited from serving as president if they have held their positions six months prior to the election.

If the president dies or vacates office, the order of succession is spelled out in Article 242 of the 1982 constitution. The presidential designates are the first three potential successors; the National Congress elects one to exercise executive power for the remainder of the presidential term. The president of the National Congress and the president of the Supreme Court of Justice are the fourth and fifth successors, respectively. During a temporary absence, the president may call upon one of the presidential designates to replace him.

The president, who is the representative of the Honduran state, has a vast array of powers as head of the executive branch. The constitution delineates forty-five presidential powers and responsibilities. The president has the responsibility to comply with and enforce the constitution, treaties and conventions, laws, and other provisions of Honduran law. He or she directs the polices of the state and fully appoints and dismisses secretaries and deputy secretaries of the cabinet and other high-ranking officials and employees (including governors of the eighteen departments) whose appointment is not assigned to other authorities.

To be elected to the National Congress, one must be a Honduran by birth who enjoys the rights of citizenship and is at least twenty-one years old. There are a number of restrictions regarding eligibility for election to the National Congress. Certain government officials and relatives of officials are not eligible if the position was held six months prior to the election. All officials or employees of the executive and judicial branches, except teachers and health-care workers, are prohibited from being elected, as are active duty members of any armed force, highranking officials of the decentralized institutions, members of the TNE, the attorney general and deputy attorney general, the comptroller general, and the director and deputy director of administrative probity. Spouses and relatives (fourth degree by blood and second degree by marriage) of certain high ranking civilian officials and certain military officials are also prohibited from serving in the National Congress, as are delinquent debtors of the National Treasury.

The nine principal justices and seven alternates on the Supreme Court of Justice are elected by the National Congress for a term of four years concomitant with the presidential and legislative terms of office. The National Congress also selects a president for the Supreme Court, and justices may be reelected. To be eligible, a justice must be Honduran by birth, a lawyer, a member of the bar association, more than thirty-five years of age, enjoy the rights of citizenship, and have held the post of trial judge or a judge on a court of appeals for at least five years.

Since the country returned to civilian democratic rule in 1982, national elections in Honduras have been held every four years for the presidency, the National Congress, and municipal officials. As provided for in the constitution and in the country's Electoral and Political Organizations Law, the National Elections Tribunal (Tribunal Nacional de Elecciones TNE) is an autonomous and independent body, with jurisdiction throughout the country and with responsibility for the organization and conduct of elections. The composition of the TNE consists of one principal member and an alternate proposed by the Supreme Court, and one principal member and an alternate proposed by each of the four registered political parties, the PLH, the PNH, the Pinu, and the PDCH. The presidency of the tribunal rotates among the members, with a term lasting one year. The TNE also names members of Departmental Elections Tribunals and Local Elections Tribunals, each with representatives from the four legally inscribed parties. The TNE has numerous rights and responsibilities, including inscribing political parties and candidates, registering voters, resolving electoral complaints, establishing the time and places for voting, training poll workers, and counting and reporting votes.

The National Registry of Persons, a dependency of the TNE, is responsible for issuing to all Hondurans exclusive identity cards, which also serve as voter registration cards, and for preparing the National Electoral Census at least five months before an election. All Hondurans are required by law to register with the National Registry of Persons.

According to some observers, a fundamental problem with the TNE is its politicization. Observers charge that the staffs of both the TNE and the National Registry of Persons are predominantly composed of political appointees with little competence or commitment. Representation is skewed toward the party in power because of the representative proposed by the Supreme Court, which essentially is a representative of the government in power. In 1985 President Suazo Córdova brazenly used the TNE to attempt to support unrepresentative factions of the two major parties. Military leader General Walter López Reyes impeded Suazo Córdova's attempt by modifying the electoral system so that party primaries and the general elections were held at the same time. The winner would be the leading candidate of the party receiving the most votes. As a result, PLH candidate José Azcona Hoyo was elected president by receiving just 25 percent of the vote, compared with the PNH candidate, Rafael Leonardo Callejas Romero, who received 45 percent. Subsequently, however, for the 1989 elections, separate party primaries were required to elect the candidates, resulting in just one candidate from each party.

As the 1993 electoral campaign got underway, the PLH made numerous charges that the National Electoral Census did not include the names of many of its party members. Despite the charges, observers maintained that the elections would probably be as legitimate as the past four elections (Constituent Assembly elections in 1980 and national elections in 1981, 1985, and 1989), which were conducted without serious irregularities.

Political Parties

Two Traditionally Dominant Parties

Honduras essentially has had two dominant political parties, the PNH and the PLH, for most of this century, with the military allying itself with the PNH for an extended period beginning in 1963. The PLH was established in 1891 under the leadership of Policarpo Bonilla Vásquez and had origins in the liberal reform efforts of the late nineteenth century. The PNH was formed in 1902 by Manuel Bonilla as a splinter group of the PLH. Between 1902 and 1948, these two parties were the only officially recognized parties, a factor that laid the foundation for the currently entrenched

PNH (red) and PLH (blue) two-party system. In the early 1990s, the internal workings of the two traditional political parties appeared to be largely free of military influence. Since the country returned to civilian rule in 1982, the military has not disrupted the constitutional order by usurping power as it did in 1956, 1963, and 1972, and it no longer appears to favor one party over the other as it did with the PNH for many years.

There appear to be few ideological differences between the two traditional parties. The PLH, or at least factions of the PLH, formerly espoused an antimilitarist stance, particularly because of the PNH's extended alliance with the military. The two PLH presidencies of the 1980s, however, appeared to end the PLH's antipathy toward the military. According to political scientists Ronald H. McDonald and J. Mark Ruhl, both parties are patron-client networks more interested in amassing political patronage than in offering effective programs. As observed by political scientist Mark Rosenberg, Honduran politicians emphasize competition and power, not national problem-solving, and governing in Honduras is determined by personal authority and power instead of institutions. The objective of political competition between the two parties has not been a competition for policies or programs, but rather a competition for personal gain in which the public sector is turned into private benefit. Nepotism is widespread and is an almost institutionalized characteristic of the political system, whereby public jobs are considered rewards for party and personal loyalty rather than having anything to do with the public trust. The practice of using political power for personal gain also helps explain how corruption appears to have become a permanent characteristic not only of the political system, but also of private enterprise.

Despite these characteristics, the two traditional parties have retained the support of the majority of the population. Popular support for the two traditional parties has been largely based on family identification, with, according to political scientist Donald Schulz, voting patterns passed on from generation to generation.

According to McDonald and Ruhl, about 60 percent of voters are identified with the traditional parties, with the PLH having a 5 percent advantage over the PNH.

Traditionally, the PNH has had a stronger constituency in rural areas and in the less developed and southern agricultural departments, whereas the PLH has been traditionally stronger in the urban areas and in the more developed northern departments, although the party has had some rural strongholds. In a study of five Honduran elections from 1957 to 1981, James Morris observes that the PLH had a strong base of support in the five departments that made up the so-called central zone of the country Atlántida, Cortés, Francisco Morazán, El Paraíso, and Yoro. The PNH had strong support in the more rural and isolated departments of Copán, Lempira, Intibucá, and Gracias a Dios, and the southern agricultural departments of Valle and Choluteca.

Looking more closely at the four national elections since 1980, one notices two facts: the PLH dominated the elections of 1980, 1981 and 1985, at times capturing departments considered PNH bulwarks (Choluteca and Valle), whereas the PNH crushed the PLH in the 1989 elections, winning all but two departments, one the traditional PLH stronghold of El Paraíso. Honduran scholar Julio Navarro has examined electoral results since 1980 and observes that in the 1989 elections the PNH won significantly not only at the department level but also at the municipal level. Of the 289 municipalities in 1989, the PNH captured 217, or about 75 percent of the country's municipalities.

According to political analysts, two significant factors helped bring about the success of the PNH in the 1989 elections: the cohesiveness and unity of the PNH and the disorder and internal factionalism of the PLH. The PLH has had a tradition of factionalism and internal party disputes. In the early 1980s, there were two formal factions: the conservative Rodista Liberal Movement (Movimiento Liberal Rodista MLR), named for deceased party leader Modesto Rodas Alvarado and controlled by Roberto Suazo Córdova; and the center-left Popular Liberal Alliance (Alianza Liberal del Pueblo Alipo), founded by brothers Carlos Roberto Reina and Jorge Arturo Reina. By 1985, however, there were five different factions of the PLH. Alipo had split with the Reina brothers to form the Revolutionary Liberal Democratic Movement (Movimiento Liberal Democrático Revolucionario M-Lider), which represented a more strongly antimilitary platform, and another faction led by newspaper publisher Jaime Rosenthal retained the Alipo banner. The MLR split into three factions: one led by President Suazo Córdova, which supported Oscar Mejía Arellano as a 1985 presidential candidate; a second faction headed by Efraín Bu Girón, who also became a presidential candidate; and a third faction led by José Azcona Hoyo, who ultimately was elected president with the support of Alipo, which did not run a candidate. Only the complicated electoral process utilized in the 1985 elections, which combined party primaries and the general election, allowed the PLH to maintain control of the government.

Three PNH factions also vied for the presidency in the 1985 elections, but the National Movement of Rafael Callejas (Movimiento Nacionalista Rafael Callejas Monarca) easily triumphed over factions led by Juan Pablo Urrutia and Fernando Lardizabel, with Callejas winning 45 percent of the total national vote and almost 94 percent of the PNH vote. PNH unity around the leadership of Callejas endured through the 1989 elections. Callejas was responsible for modernizing the organization of the PNH and incorporating diverse social and economic sectors into the party. As a result, in the 1989 elections he was able to break the myth of PLH inviolability that had been established in the three previous elections of the 1980s. In the 1989 contest, the PNH broke PLH strongholds throughout the country.

The PLH was not as successful as the PNH in achieving party unity for the 1989 elections. The PLH candidate, Carlos Flores Facusse, had survived a bruising four-candidate party primary in December 1988 in which he received 35.5 percent of the total vote.

As noted by Julio Navarro, Flores was an extremely vulnerable candidate because in the primary he did not win major urban areas or departments considered PLH strongholds.

The electoral campaign for the November 1993 national elections was well underway by mid-1993. The PLH nominated Carlos Roberto Reina Idiáquez, a founder of M-Lider and former president of the Inter-American Court of Human Rights (IACHR), the leftist PLH faction. The PNH nominated conservative and controversial Osvaldo Ramos Soto, former Supreme Court president and former rector of the UNAH in the 1980s. As of mid-1993, public opinion polls showed the two candidates about even.

Reina won his party's nomination in elections on December 6, 1992, by capturing 47.5 percent of the vote in a six-candidate primary; second place was taken by newspaper publisher Rosenthal, who received 26.1 percent of the vote. Unlike the PLH primary of December 1988, the 1992 PLH nomination process demonstrated the party's strong support for Reina, who won in fourteen out of eighteen departments. Reina, who represented Honduras before the International Court of Justice (ICJ) in the border conflict with El Salvador, advocated a "moral revolution" in the country and vowed to punish those who enriched themselves through corruption.

The nomination process for the PNH was not an open process like that of the PLH, and a vote scheduled for November 29, 1993, served only to legalize the candidacy of Ramos Soto. The actual process of choosing the PNH candidate had occurred several months earlier, in July 1992, when the Monarca faction and the Ramos Soto faction struck a deal in which Ramos Soto was to be the candidate. The Monarca's presidential precandidate, Nora Gunera de Melgar (the widow of General Juan Alberto Melgar Castro, former head of state), was eliminated from consideration despite her objections. Other minor factions were not allowed to present their candidates.

In his campaign, Ramos Soto described himself as a "successful peasant" ("*campesino superado*"), alluding to his humble origins in order to gain popular support. Despite capturing the nomination, Ramos Soto encountered some resistance to his PNH candidacy, with some party members believing that his election would be a setback for the modernization program begun by President Callejas. Other Honduran sectors remembered Ramos Soto's reign as UNAH rector when he led a campaign to oust leftist student groups. Some human rights activists even claimed that Ramos Soto had collaborated with the military to assassinate leftists at the university.

Smaller Political Parties and Movements

Since Honduras's return to civilian democratic rule in the 1980s, two small centrist political parties, the Pinu and the PDCH, have participated in regular national presidential and legislative elections. Neither party, however, has challenged the political domination of the two traditional parties. Both parties have received most of their support from urban centers of Tegucigalpa and San Pedro Sula, Choluteca, and La Ceiba. In the presidential elections of 1981, 1985, and 1989, Pinu received 2.5 percent, 1.4 percent, and 1.8 percent, respectively, and the PDCH received 1.6 percent, 1.9 percent, and 1.4 percent. Both parties have presented presidential candidates for the 1993 national elections.

Pinu was first organized in 1970 by businessman Miguel Andonie Fernández as an effort to reform and reinvigorate the nation's political life. This urban-based group, which draws support from middle-class professionals, first attempted to gain legal recognition (*personería jurídica*) in 1970, but the PNH blocked Pinu's attempts until the 1980 Constituent Assembly elections. Pinu won three seats in those elections, important because only two votes separated the two traditional parties in the National Congress. Pinu also held a cabinet position in the provisional government headed by General Policarpo Paz García (1980-82) in 1980. In the 1981 elections, Pinu acquired three legislative seats, whereas in the 1985 and 1989 elections it won only two seats. Pinu became affiliated with the Social Democratic International in 1988. In 1985 and 1989, Enrique Aguilar Cerrato was the Pinu presidential candidate, and in 1993 businessperson Olban Valladares was the party's candidate.

The origins of the Honduras Christian Democratic Party (Partido Demócrata de Honduras PDCH) date back to the 1960s, when, in the wake of Vatican Council II, the Roman Catholic Church became involved in the development of community organizations, including unions, and student and peasant groups. In 1968 lay persons associated with the Roman Catholic Church founded the Christian Democratic Movement of Honduras (Movimiento Demócrata Cristiano de Honduras MDCH), which in 1975 became the PDCH. According to Mark Rosenberg, the party became more progressive than the Roman Catholic Church and maintained solid ties with peasant organizations. Although the party applied for legal recognition, the PNH blocked the process, and the party did not receive recognition until late 1980, too late to be part of the Constituent Assembly drafting a new constitution, but just in time to compete in the 1981 national elections. In those elections, the PDCH earned just one seat in the National Congress. In the 1985 elections, the party won two seats in the National Congress, but in 1989 it did not win any representation. Efraín Díaz Arrivillaga, who reportedly gave the party the reputation for being the "conscience" of the Honduran National Congress in the 1980s, was the PDCH's 1989 presidential candidate; the 1993 candidate was businessperson Marcos Orlando Iriarte Arita.

In the early 1980s, amidst the Sandinista revolution in Nicaragua and the civil conflict in El Salvador, several radical leftist guerrilla groups that advocated some type of armed action against the Honduran government were formed in Honduras. The Honduran Revolutionary Party of Central American Workers (Partido Revolucionario de los Trabajadores Centroaméricanos de Honduras PRTCH) was formed in 1976 as part of a regional party. The Morazanist Front for the Liberation of Honduras (Frente

Morazanista para la Liberación de Honduras FMLH), first active in 1980, was named for Honduran national hero Francisco Morazán, who had tried to keep the Central American states unified in the early nineteenth century. The Lorenzo Zelaya Popular Revolutionary Forces (Fuerzas Populares Revolucionarias Lorenzo Zelaya FPR-LZ), founded in 1980 and named for a communist peasant leader who was murdered in 1965, traced its roots to a pro- Chinese faction of the PCH. The Cinchoneros Popular Liberation Movement (Movimiento Popular de Liberación Cinchoneros MPLC), founded in 1981, was named for a nineteenth century peasant leader. With the exception of the MPLC which had about 300 members, the groups had memberships of fewer than 100 participants each.

In 1982 these new radical groups joined the Communist Party of Honduras (Partido Comunista de Honduras PCH), under the loose umbrella of the National Unified Directorate-Movement of Revolutionary Unity (Directorio Nacional Unificado-Movimiento de Unidad Revolucionario DNU-MUR). The PCH, which was formed in 1927, had been the country's major leftist opposition group through the 1970s, but had rarely resorted to violence before its affiliation with the DNU-MUR. An offshoot of the PCH that was not part of the DNU-MUR was the Marxist-Leninist Communist Party of Honduras (Partido Comunista Marxista-Leninista de Honduras PCMLH), formed in 1967 by PCH dissidents.

Guerrilla groups in Honduras were responsible for numerous terrorist incidents throughout the 1980s. These included a successful plane hijacking in exchange for the freeing of political prisoners, the holding of hostages, bombings, and attacks against United States military personnel and advisers. Political assassinations included the January 1989 murder of General Gustavo lvarez Martinez by the members of the MPLC. Nevertheless, compared with neighboring El Salvador and Nicaragua, these groups were small and did not attract much popular support. According to analysts, one fundamental reason is the conservative nature of Honduran society, which is not conducive to a revolutionary uprising. Moreover, according to political scientist Donald Schulz, Honduran society is characterized by a network of interlocking interest groups and political organizations that have reconciled conflicts that could have turned violent. Schulz also observes that important escape valves like agrarian reform, a strong union movement, an entrenched two-party system, and the restoration of elected democracy in the 1980s also enabled Honduras to escape the revolution of its neighbors.

Some analysts maintain that another important factor explaining why revolutionary groups did not gain much ground in Honduras was the government's swift use of repression. In the early 1980s, when General was military chief, the military waged a campaign against leftist groups that included political assassinations, disappearances, and illegal detentions. Those leftist political leaders who escaped the military's campaign did so by going into exile. In the summer of 1983, the military struck against the PRTCH, which reportedly was moving a contingent of almost 100 guerrillas into the Honduran province of Olancho from Nicaragua. The Honduran military claimed that most of the rebels were killed in combat or died from exhaustion while hiding out from the military, but human rights organizations maintain that most of the rebels, including a United States-born Jesuit priest, James Carney, were detained and executed.

With the end of the Contra war in Nicaragua in 1990 and a peace accord in El Salvador in 1991, Honduran guerrilla groups lost important sources of support. By 1992 most guerrilla groups, including the six groups of the DNU-MUR, had largely ceased operating, and many political exiles had returned to the country in order to take advantage of an amnesty offered by the Callejas government. Some former exiles worked to establish new political parties. For example, the PCMLH formed the Party for the Transformation of Honduras (Partido para la Transformación de Honduras PTH), and the FMLH established the Morazanist Liberation Party (Partido Morazanista de Liberación PML). Other leftist groups operating openly in the early 1990s included the Honduran Revolutionary Party (Partido Revolucionario Hondureño

PRH), the Workers' Party (Partido de los Trabajadores PT), the Patriotic Renovation Party (Partido de Renovación Patriótica PRP), and the People's Democratic Movement (Movimiento Democrático del Pueblo MDP).

These six parties, which reportedly planned to run under a united front in 1998 elections, presented a plan to President Callejas in 1992 to reform the country's electoral law in order to facilitate the participation of smaller parties in national elections; the plan included a reduction of signatures required for a party to be legally registered. In order to be legally registered, a political party must complete a complex process that can be made even more complex by the politicization of the electoral tribunal. A party seeking legal recognition, according to the nation's Electoral and Political Organizations Law, must have local organizations in at least half of the nation's departments and municipalities, and must present valid nominations of at least 20,000 registered voters affiliated with the party asking to be registered.

Despite the incorporation of most leftist leaders and groups into the political system, there were still sporadic terrorist actions in Honduras in the early 1990s instigated by remnants or factions of the armed guerrilla groups of the 1980s. For example, although four top leaders of the Cinchoneros renounced armed struggle in May 1991, a faction of the group still wanted to fight and was responsible for the burning of an electric company building in 1992. Moreover, a small fringe group known as the Morazanist Patriotic Front, which appeared to be unrelated to the FMLH, vowed to continue armed struggle and claimed responsibility for terrorist attacks and several political killings in the early 1990s.

At various times during the 1980s, there were also reports of the presence of right-wing extremist groups, which were associated with the Honduran military. Most observers judged that the military and police were largely responsible for right-wing extremism throughout the 1980s. In the early 1980s, when the military was under the command of General Álvarez, reportedly more than 140 disappearances of government opponents were carried out, largely by a secret army unit, or death squad apparatus, known as Battalion 3- 16. For the balance of the 1980s, the military and police were reportedly involved in extrajudicial killings of opponents and torture, but not at the high level of the first part of the decade. In 1988 and 1989, a paramilitary group known as the Alliance for Anticommunist Action (Alianza de Acción Anticomunista AAA), which human rights organizations contend was tied to the military, was involved in a campaign to intimidate leftist leaders and human rights activists. The AAA took credit for several activities aimed at intimidating the left and human rights groups, including making death threats, circulating threatening posters with the AAA logo, and defacing property.

Interest Groups

In the early 1990s, Honduras had a variety of interest groups that influenced the political process, some more successfully than others. Although Honduran political tradition is characterized by a strong executive, political scientist Donald Schulz maintains that the society is characterized by an elaborate network of interest groups and political organizations that help resolve conflicts. According to Schulz, the essence of Honduran politics is the struggle within and among competing groups, with public decisions arrived at through the long process of consensusbuilding .

Business Organizations

According to Mark Rosenberg, the private sector in Honduras has historically been one of the weakest in Central America because of the economy's domination by foreign-owned banana companies. The private sector, however, got a boost in the 1960s with the creation of the Central American Common Market (CACM see Appendix B). In 1967 the Honduran Private Enterprise

Council (Consejo Hondureño de la Empresa Privada Cohep) was established to serve as an umbrella organization for most private-sector business organizations.

In the early 1980s, a short-lived business organization, the Association for the Progress of Honduras (Asociación para el Progreso de Honduras Aproh), was formed during the presidency of Suazo Córdova; it was headed by armed forces commander General lvarez. Aproh, which was made up of conservative business leaders, had an anticommunist bent, and appeared to be a means for General lvarez to establish a power base outside the military. It received a US$50,000 contribution from a front group for the Unification Church, led by the Reverend Sun Myung Moon, which had begun to proselytize in Honduras. The existence of Aproh appeared to be directly tied to the fate of General Álvarez, and as a result, when he was ousted in 1984, Aproh lost its source of support and fell into disarray. Moreover, the Roman Catholic Church in Honduras denounced the dangers posed by the Unification Church (whose members were referred to as Moonies), a measure that was a further setback to the fate of Aproh. In the 1993 presidential elections, Aproh received media attention because PNH presidential candidate Osvaldo Ramos Soto had been a prominent member of Aproh, coordinating its Committee for the Defense and Support of Democratic Institutions. Human rights groups in Honduras claimed that Aproh was associated with the political killings and disappearances of leftist activists during the early 1980s.

In the early 1990s, Cohep was the most important businesssector interest group, representing about thirty private-sector organizations. Essentially an organization of the business elite that tries to influence government policy, the group has often been used as a business sounding board when the government is considering new policy initiatives. Within Cohep, several organizations stand out as the most powerful; they often issue their own statements or positions on the government's economic policy. Among these, the Cortés Chamber of Commerce and Industry (Cámara de Comercio e

Industrias de Cortés CCIC), which represents the private sector of San Pedro Sula, was originally formed in 1931, but was restructured in 1951 and since then has served as a strong development proponent and vocal advocate for the northern coastal region of the country. Another body, the National Association of Industrialists (Asociación Nacional de Industriales- -ANDI), was a vocal critic of the Callejas administration's liberalization program designed to open the Honduran market to outside competition. Another group, the Tegucigalpa Chamber of Commerce and Industry (Cámara de Comercio de Industrias de Tegucigalpa CCIT), supported the government's trade liberalization efforts.

Overlapping with Cohep membership is the National Federation of Agriculturists and Stockraisers of Honduras (Federación Nacional de Agricultores y Ganaderos de Honduras Fenagh). Founded in the 1960s, it has been an active opponent of land reform, and in 1975 was responsible for the killing of several people, including two priests, in a peasant training center in Olancho department. Fenagh strongly supported a new agricultural modernization law approved by the Honduran National Congress in 1992 that was opposed by most peasant organizations. Another organization that overlaps with Cohep's membership is the Honduran Federation of Chambers of Commerce and Industry (Federación de Cámaras de Comercio e Industrias de Honduras), founded in 1988, which functions largely as a service organization for its members throughout the country.

The private sector in Honduras is divided by a variety of rivalries. These rivalries include the traditional competition between Tegucigalpa and San Pedro Sula and the animosity between *turco* (Arab immigrants who arrived early in this century carrying Ottoman Empire Turkish travel documents) entrepreneurs and native-born Honduran entrepreneurs. Divisions were also apparent in the early 1990s, in conjunction with the trade liberalization efforts initiated by the Callejas government. Those business sectors able to compete with imported goods and services supported liberalization measures, whereas those producers more dependent on government protection or subsidies opposed the trade liberalization program.

Labor and Peasant Organizations

The organized labor movement of Honduras, traditionally the strongest in Central America, first began organizing in the early years of the twentieth century. The movement, however, gained momentum only with the great banana strike of 1954, at which point organized labor unions became a political force in the country, at times having an important impact on government policy. In that year, labor won the right to form unions legally and to engage in collective bargaining. In addition, the country's first national peasant organizations were formed in the mid-1950s, and later picked up momentum when an Agrarian Reform Law was enacted in 1962.

In the early 1990s, trade unions represented about 20 percent of the Honduran labor force and exerted considerable economic and political influence. According to the United States Department of State's 1992 human rights report, unions frequently participated in public rallies against government policies and made use of the media. Unions also gained wage and other concessions from employers through collective bargaining and the use of the right to strike. For example, in May 1992, direct negotiations between organized labor and the private sector led to a 13.7 percent increase in the minimum wage, the third consecutive annual increase.

Nevertheless, organized unions and peasant organizations still experienced significant difficulties in the early 1990s. Retribution against workers for trade union activity was not uncommon and the right to bargain collectively was not always guaranteed. Union activists at times were the target of political violence, including assassination, and workers were at times harassed or fired for their trade union activities. Several peasant leaders were killed for political reasons; and in a highly publicized

May 1991 massacre, five members of a peasant organization were killed, reportedly by military members, because of a land dispute. The government also at times supported pro- government parallel unions over elected unions in an attempt to quiet labor unrest.

In 1993 Honduras had three major labor confederations: the Confederation of Honduran Workers (Confederación de Trabajadores de Honduras CTH), claiming a membership of about 160,000 workers; the General Workers' Central (Central General de Trabajadores CGT), claiming to represent 120,000 members; and the Unitary Confederation of Honduran Workers (Confederación Unitaria de Trabajadores de Honduras CUTH), a new confederation formed in May 1992, with an estimated membership of about 30,000. The three confederations included numerous trade union federations, individual unions, and peasant organizations.

The CTH, the nation's largest trade confederation, was formed in 1964 by the nation's largest peasant organization, the National Association of Honduran Peasants (Asociación Nacional de Campesinos de Honduras Anach), and by Honduran unions affiliated with the Inter-American Regional Organization of Workers (Organización Regional Interamericana de Trabajadores ORIT), a hemispheric labor organization with close ties to the American Federation of Labor and Congress of Industrial Organization (AFL-CIO). In the early 1990s, the confederation had three major components, the 45,000- member Federation of Unions of National Workers of Honduras (Federación Sindical de Trabajadores Nacionales de Honduras Fesitranh), the 22,000-member Central Federation of Honduran Free Trade Unions (Federación Central de Sindicatos Libres de Honduras), and the 2,200-member Federation of National Maritime Unions of Honduras (Federación de Sindicales Marítimas Nacionales de Honduras). In addition, Anach, claiming to represent between 60,000-80,000 members, was affiliated with Fesitranh. Fesitranh was by far the country's most powerful labor federation, with most of its unions located in San Pedro Sula and the Puerto Cortés Free Zone. The unions of the United States-owned banana companies and the United States-owned petroleum refinery also were affiliated with Fesitranh. The CTH received support from foreign labor organizations, including ORIT; the American Institute for Free Labor Development (AIFLD); and Germany's Friedreich Ebert Foundation. The CTH was an affiliate of the International Confederation of Free Trade Unions (ICFTU).

The CGT, first formed in 1970, but not legally recognized until 1982, was originally formed by the Christian Democrats and received external support from the World Confederation of Labor (WCL) and the Latin American Workers Central (Central Latinoamericana de Trabajadores CLAT), a regional organization supported by Christian Democratic parties. In the late 1980s and early 1990s, however, the CGT leadership developed close ties to the PNH, and several leaders served in the Callejas government. Another national peasant organization, the National Union of Peasants (Unión Nacional de Campesinos UNC), claiming a membership of 40,000, has been affiliated with the CGT for many years and is a principal force within the confederation.

The CUTH was formed in May 1992 by two principal labor federations, the Unitary Federation of Honduran Workers (Federación Unitaria de Trabajadores de Honduras FUTH) and the Independent Federation of Honduran Workers (Federación Independiente de Trabajadores de Honduras FITH), as well as several smaller labor groups, all critical of the Callejas government's strong neoliberal economic reform program. The Marxist FUTH, with an estimated 16,000 members in the early 1990s, was first organized in 1980 by three communist-influenced unions, but did not receive legal status until 1988. The federation had external ties with the World Federation of Trade Unions (WFTU), the Permanent Congress for Latin American Workers Trade Union Unity (Congreso Permanente de Unidad Sindical de Trabajadores de América Latina CPUSTAL), and the Central American Committee of Trade Union Unity (Comité de Unidad Sindical de Centroamérica CUSCA). Its affiliations included water utility, university, electricity company, brewery, and teacher unions, as well as several peasant organizations, including the National Central of Farm Workers (Central Nacional de Trabajadores del Campo CNTC), formed in 1985 and active in land occupations in the early 1980s.

FUTH also became affiliated with a number of leftist popular organizations in a group known as the Coordinating Committee of Popular Organizations (Comité Coordinadora de las Organizaciones Populares CCOP) that was formed in 1984. The FITH, claiming about 13,000 members in the early 1990s, was granted legal status in 1988. Originally formed by dissident FUTH members, the federation consisted of fourteen unions.

Many Honduran peasant organizations were affiliated with the three labor confederations in the early 1990s. Anach was created and received legal recognition in 1962 in order to counter the communist-influenced peasant movement of the National Federation of Honduran Peasants (Federación Nacional de Campesinos de Honduras   Fenach). In contrast, Fenach never received legal recognition. Its offices were destroyed following the 1963 military coup by Colonel Oswaldo López Arellano, and, in 1965, seven of Fenach's leaders who had taken up armed struggle against the government, including founder Lorenzo Zelaya, were killed by the military. Anach became the primary peasant organization and in 1967 became affiliated with the CTH.

The UNC, traditionally a principal rival of Anach and traditionally more radical than Anach, was established in 1970 but did not receive legal recognition until 1984. The UNC traces its roots to the community development organizations and peasant leagues established by the Roman Catholic Church in the 1960s. The UNC was a founding member of the CGT and had ideological ties to the MDCH.

In addition to Anach and the UNC, another large peasant organization in the 1990s was the Honduran Federation of Agrarian Reform Cooperatives (Federación de Cooperativas de la Reforma

Agraria de Honduras Fecorah). The federation was formed in 1970 and received legal recognition in 1974. In the early 1990s, Fecorah had about 22,000 members.

There were numerous attempts to unify the nation's peasant organizations in the 1970s and 1980s, but the sector was characterized by numerous divisions, including ideological divisions. For some peasant organizations, political affiliation changed with changes in the government. Disillusionment with the neglect of unions and peasant organizations under the PLH administrations of the 1980s caused some groups to move toward the PNH. In 1988 the three major peasant organizations, Anach, the UNC, and Fecorah, along with smaller leftist peasant groupings, united under the banner of the Coordinating Council of Honduran Peasant Organizations (Consejo Coordinador de Organizaciones Campesinas de Honduras Cocoh) to lobby for agrarian reform. Just four years later, however, in May 1992, the peasant movement was split by disagreement over the Callejas government's proposed agricultural modernization law. The three major peasant organizations all left Cocoh to form the National Peasants Council (Consejo Nacional de Campesinos CNC), while leftist peasant organizations remained in Cocoh and actively demonstrated against the proposed agricultural modernization law.

From 1989 until 1992, the nation's major peasant organizations and labor federations, a confederation of cooperatives, and several professional organizations supported the "Platform of Struggle for the Democratization of Honduras." The objective of the campaign was to present far-reaching economic, social, and political reform proposals to the national government, which included issuing several documents and a manifesto. By 1993 however, this initiative had disappeared because of divisions among the disparate groups and, according to some observers, because of the Callejas government's success in coopting several organizations.

The organized peasant movement in Honduras was an important, if not determinant, factor in implementing an agrarian reform program. In the early 1960s, because of increasing pressure on the government from landless peasants and external pressure from the United States through the Alliance for Progress, the PLH government of Ramón Villeda Morales took significant steps toward implementing a land reform program. He established the National Agrarian Institute (Instituto Nacional Agrario INA) in 1961 and the following year approved an agrarian reform law that especially was aimed at the uncultivated lands of the United States-owned fruit companies. The 1963 military coup and subsequent repressive rule of General López Arellano brought an abrupt halt to land redistribution. By the late 1960s, however, peasant organizations were again increasing pressure on the government, and under a director who was sympathetic to the peasant movement, the INA began to adjudicate land claims in favor of peasants.

The election of conservative Ramón Ernesto Cruz as president in 1971 once again shifted the government's agrarian policy to one favoring the large landholders, but with the 1972 coup, again led by General López Arellano, the government instituted a far-reaching agrarian reform program. The program was all the more significant because it was driven by López Arellano, who had crushed land reform efforts in the 1960s. This time around, however, the general allied himself with peasant organizations. He issued an emergency land reform decree in 1972 and in 1975 issued another agrarian reform measure that promised to distribute 600,000 hectares to 120,000 families over a period of approximately five years.

In 1975, however, a conservative countercoup by General Juan Melgar Castro ended these high expectations for land redistribution. After 1977 land redistribution continued, but at lower levels. According to a study by Charles Brockett, from 1962 through 1984, a little more than 293,000 hectares were distributed, benefiting about 52,000 families countrywide. Brockett observed, however, that most of the land distributed was public land rather than idle or underutilized private land. In the 1980s, land redistribution slowed while peasant land takeovers of underused land continued unabated. The government's reaction to the takeovers was mixed. At times, the military reversed them by force, and, on other occasions, the government did nothing to stop the occupations.

In 1992 the Callejas government enacted a new agricultural modernization law that some observers claim essentially ended prospects for additional land distribution. The law, approved by the National Congress in March 1992, limited expropriations and augmented guarantees for private ownership of land. The United States Department of State observed that the law improved the environment for increases in investment, production, and agricultural exports. The law was actively opposed by some peasant organizations, who waged a campaign of land occupations and claimed that those peasant organizations that supported the law were linked to PNH or were bought by the government.

In the early 1990s, the government increasingly intervened in the affairs of labor unions and peasant organizations through parallel unions. For example, in July 1992, the Callejas government gave legal recognition to two parallel unions in the telecommunications workers union and to a second union representing road, airport, and terminal maintenance employees. In October 1992, the government recognized a faction of Anach that favored the Callejas government's proposed agricultural modernization law even though another faction had won a union election.

Unions in Honduras have strongly opposed the growth of solidarity (*solidarismo*) associations, which emphasize labor-management harmony. These associations, which consist of representatives of both labor and management, provide a variety of services by utilizing a joint worker/employer capital fund. Solidarity associations began in the late 1940s in Costa Rica and have thrived there, accounting for almost 16 percent of the work force. In Honduras solidarity associations first appeared in 1985 and, although the government had not granted the associations legal status, by the early 1990s they accounted for about 10,000 workers in a variety of companies. Organized labor, including Honduran unions and international labor affiliations, strongly opposes solidarity associations on the grounds that they do not permit the right to strike and that they do not include appropriate grievance procedures. Unions contend that the associations are management- controlled mechanisms that undermine unionism. In 1991 a bitter strike at El Mochito mine was reportedly begun by unions who opposed management's attempt to impose a solidarity association there.

Popular Organizations

A plethora of special interest organizations and associations were active during the 1980s and early 1990s. Some of these organizations, like student groups and women's groups, had been active long before the 1980s, but others, such as human rights organization and environmental groups, only formed in the 1980s. Still other groups were just beginning to organize. In 1993, for example, a newly formed homosexual rights association petitioned the government for legal recognition. Beginning in 1984, a number of leftist popular organizations were linked with the FUTH in the CCOP. Some observers maintain that the number and power of popular organizations grew in the 1980s because of the inertia and manipulation associated with the traditional political process. Others contend that the proliferation of popular organizations demonstrates the free and open nature of Honduran society and the belief of the citizens that they can influence the political process by organizing.

The student movement in Honduras, which dates back to 1910, is concentrated at the country's largest institution of higherlearning , UNAH, which had an enrollment of around 30,000 students in the early 1990s. Ideological divisions among the student population and student organizations have often led to violence, including the assassination of student leaders. Leftist students, organized into the Reformist University Front (Frente de Reforma Universitaria FRU), largely dominated student organizations until the early 1980s, but ideological schisms within the group and an anti-leftist campaign orchestrated by General Gustavo Álvarez broke leftist control of official university student bodies. Since the early 1980s, the rightwing Democratic University United Front (Frente Unido Universitario Democrático FUUD), which reportedly has ties to the PNH and to the military, has become the more powerful student organization, with close ties to the conservative university administration. Osvaldo Ramos Soto, the PNH 1993 presidential candidate, served as FUUD coordinator while he was UNAH's rector in the mid-1980s. In the early 1990s, political violence in the student sector escalated. FRU leader Ramón Antonio Bricero was brutally tortured and murdered in 1990, and four FUUD activists were assassinated in the 1990-92 period.

Organized women's groups in Honduras date back to the 1920s with the formation of the Women's Cultural Society that struggled for women's economic and political rights. Visitación Padilla, who also actively opposed the intervention of the United States Marines in Honduras in 1924, and Graciela García were major figures in the women's movement. Women were also active in the formation of the Honduran labor movement and took part in the great banana strike of 1954. In the early 1950s, women's associations fought for women's suffrage, which finally was achieved in 1954, making Honduras the last Latin American country to extend voting rights to women. In the late 1970s, a national peasant organization, the Honduras Federation of Peasant Women (Federación Hondureña de Mujeres Campesinas Fehmuca), was formed; by the 1980s, it represented almost 300 organizations nationwide. As a more leftist-oriented women's peasant organization, the Council for Integrated Development of Peasant Women (Consejo de Desarrollo Integrado de Mujeres Campesinos Codeimuca) was established in the late 1980s and represented more than 100 women's groups. Another leftist women's organization, the Visitación Padilla Committee, was active in the 1980s, opposing the presence of the United States military and the Contras in Honduras.

Numerous other women's groups were active in the late 1980s and early 1990s, including a research organization known as the Honduran Center for Women's Studies (Centro de Estudios de la Mujer-Honduras CEM-H). Another organization, the Honduran Federation of Women's Associations (Federación Hondureña de Asociaciones Femininas Fehaf), represented about twenty-five women's groups and was involved in such activities as providing legal assistance to women and lobbying the government on women's issues.

Although women were represented at all levels of government in the late 1980s and early 1990s, their numbers were few. According to CEM-H, following the 1989 national elections, women held 9.4 percent of congressional seats and 6.2 percent of mayorships nationwide, including the mayorship of Tegucigalpa. In the Callejas government, women held several positions, including one seat on the Supreme Court, three out of thirty-two ambassadorships, and two out of fifty-four high-level executive branch positions. For the 1993 presidential elections, the Monarca faction of the PNH originally supported the nomination of a woman as the PNH candidate, and the PLH nominated a woman as one of its three presidential designate candidates.

Domestic Human Rights Organizations

Human rights groups in Honduras first became active in the early 1980s when revolution and counterrevolution brought violence and instability to Central America. In Honduras, these groups organized in response to the mounting level of violence targeted at leftist organizations, particularly from 1982-84, when General Gustavo lvarez commanded the military. Human rights organizations were at times targeted by the Honduran military with harassment and political violence. According to some observers, the United States embassy in Honduras also got involved in a campaign to discredit Honduran human rights organizations at a time when Honduras was serving as a key component of United States policy toward Central

America by hosting the Contras and a United States military presence.

In the early 1990s, there were three major nongovernmental human rights organizations in Honduras: the Committee for the Defense of Human Rights in Honduras (Comité para la Defensa de Derechos Humanos de Honduras Codeh); the Committee of the Families of the Detained and Disappeared in Honduras (Comité de las Familias de los Detenidos y Desaparecidos Hondureños Cofadeh); and the Center of the Investigation and Promotion of Human Rights (Centro de Investigación y Promoción de los Derechos Humanos Ciprodeh).

Established in 1981 by Ramón Custodio, Codeh became the country's foremost human rights organization in the 1980s, with a network throughout the country. The organization withstood harassment and intimidation by Honduran security forces. In January 1988, Codeh's regional director in northern Honduras, Miguel Ángel Pavón, was assassinated before he was about to testify in a case brought before the Inter-American Court of Human Rights (IACHR). In 1981 and 1982, Codeh and Cofadeh had brought three cases before the IACHR involving the disappearances of two Hondurans, Ángel Manfredo Velásquez and Saúl Godínez, and two Costa Ricans traveling in Honduras, Fairen Garbi and Yolanda Solís Corrales. The court ultimately found Honduras responsible for the disappearances of the two Hondurans, but not for the two Costa Ricans.

In the 1990s, Codeh remained the country's most important and most internationally known human rights organization. Codeh continued to issue annual reports and to speak out frequently, not only on human rights violations, but also on economic, social, and political issues. Some observers, however, have criticized Codeh for going beyond a human rights focus, as well as for exaggerating charges against the government and military. In the 1980s and as late as 1990, the United States Department of State in its annual human rights reports on Honduras charged that Codeh's charges were ill-documented, exaggerated, and in some cases false.

Cofadeh was founded in 1982 by Zenaida Velásquez, sister of Ángel Manfredo Velásquez, the missing student and labor activist whose case Codeh and Cofadeh brought before the IACHR. As its name suggests, Cofadeh's membership consisted of relatives of the disappeared and detained, and in the 1980s its members often demonstrated near the Presidential Palace in the center of Tegucigalpa.

Ciprodeh, founded in 1991 by Leo Valladares, provides human rights educational and legal services. The group offers human rights courses and monthly seminars and has a special program for the protection of the rights of children and women.

The Honduran government did not established an effective human rights monitor until late 1992, and Codeh and Cofadeh often served this purpose. In 1987 the Azcona government established the InterInstitutional Commission on Human Rights (Comisión InterInstitucional de Derechos Humanos CIDH), made up of representatives from the three branches of government and the military, to investigate human rights violations. The CIDH proved ineffective and did not receive cooperation from either civilian judicial or military authorities.

In December 1992, the Callejas government inaugurated a new governmental human rights body headed by Valladares. In 1993 this new office of the National Commission for the Protection of Human Rights (Comisión Nacional para la Protección de Derechos Humanos Conaprodeh) received complaints of human rights violations and, in some instances, provided "protection" to those citizens issuing complaints.

In the early 1990s, Honduras also had a number of ethnic-based organizations representing Hondurans of African origin and the nation's indigenous population. Six ethnic-based organizations were loosely grouped together under the Honduras Advisory Council for Autonomous Ethnic Development (Consejo Asesor Hondureño para el Desarrollo de las Étnicas Autóctonas CAHDEA). Representing the nation's black population, including the Garifuna, and English-speaking Creoles was the Honduras Black Fraternal Organization (Organización Fraternal Negra Hondureña Ofraneh), a group established in 1977 for the betterment of social, political, economic, and cultural conditions of black Hondurans. The indigenous peoples of Honduras first began forming national organizations in the 1950s, and in the 1990s, five indigenous organizations were represented in CAHDEA. These consisted of organizations representing the Miskito, Pech, Lenca, Towaka, and Jicaque peoples. According to the United States Department of State in its human rights report for 1992, Honduran indigenous peoples had "little or no participation in decisions affecting their lands, cultures, traditions, or the allocation of natural resources." The report further asserted that legal recourse is commonly denied to indigenous groups and that the seizing of indigenous lands by nonindigenous farmers and cattle growers is common.

The Press

Freedom of speech and the press are guaranteed by the Honduran constitution, and in practice these rights are generally respected. Nevertheless, as noted in the United States Department of State's 1992 human rights report, the media are subject to both corruption and politicization, and there have been instances of selfcensorship , allegations of intimidation by military authorities, and payoffs to journalists. In a scandal that came to light in January 1993, a Honduran newspaper published an internal document from the National Elections Tribunal (Tribunal Nacional de Elecciones TNE) that listed authorized payments to thirteen journalists. Observers maintain that numerous governmental institutions, including municipalities, the National Congress, the various ministries, and the military, have been involved in paying journalists for stories; some estimate that more than 50 percent of journalists receive payoffs. Another significant problem in the media has been self-censorship in reporting on sensitive issues, especially the military. Intimidation in the form of threats, blacklisting, and violence also occurred at various times in the 1980s and early 1990s.

According to some analysts, however, despite instances of military intimidation of the press in early 1993, the media, including the press, radio, and television, has played an important role in creating an environment conducive to the public's open questioning and criticism of authorities. Honduran sociologist Leticia Salomón has observed that in early 1993 the media, including newspaper caricatures, played an instrumental role in mitigating the fear of criticizing the military, and he asserts that this diminishment of fear was an important step in the building of a democratic culture in Honduras.

Honduras has five daily national newspapers, three based in Tegucigalpa *El Periódico*, *La Tribuna* and *El Heraldo* and two based in San Pedro Sula *El Tiempo* and *La Prensa*. Quite conservative in its outlook, *El Periódico* has former president Callejas as its principal stockholder. Owned by PLH leader and businessperson Jaime Rosenthal (who placed second in the PLH presidential primary for the 1993 national election), the left-of-center *El Tiempo* has been the newspaper most prone to criticize the police and military, for which its editor, Manuel Gamero, has at times been jailed. In February 1993, a bomb exploded at the home of the newspaper's business manager after the paper gave refuge to a reporter, Eduardo Coto, who had witnessed the assassination of a San Pedro Sula businessperson, Eduardo Pina, in late January 1993. Coto alleged that Pina had been killed by two former members of the notorious Battalion 3-16, a military unit reportedly responsible for numerous disappearances in the early 1980s. After alleged death threats from military members, Coto fled to Spain, where he received asylum.

La Tribuna and *La Prensa* are considered centrist papers by some observers, although some might put *La Prensa* into the more conservative center-right category. *La Tribuna*, which is owned by Carlos Flores Facusse (the unsuccessful 1989 presidential candidate), has close ties to the PLH and to the new industrial sector of Tegucigalpa. *La Prensa* has close ties with the business section of San Pedro Sula. Its president and editor is Jorge Canahuati Larach, whose family also publishes *El Heraldo*, a conservative paper that has been more favorable to the military in its reporting than other dailies and often reflects the positions of the PNH.

In addition to the five dailies, Honduras also has numerous smaller publications. Most significantly, the Honduran Documentation Center (Centro de Documentación de Honduras Cedoh), run by the widely respected political analyst Victor Meza, publishes a monthly *Boletín Informativo*; and Cedoh and the sociology department of UNAH publish *Puntos de Vista*, a magazine dedicated to social and political analysis. In addition, an English-language weekly paper, *Honduras This Week*, covers events in Honduras and in Central America.

Civilian Democratic Rule

In the decade since Honduras returned to civilian democratic rule in 1982, the political system has undergone notable changes. Hondurans successfully elected three civilian presidents in the 1980s, and elections came to be celebrated in an almost holidaylike atmosphere, similar to the electoral process in Costa Rica. In 1993 the nation was again gearing up for national elections in November, with conservative Osvaldo Ramos Soto of the PNH squaring off against Carlos Roberto Reina, leader of a leftist faction of the PLH. Although remaining a powerful factor in the political system, the military is increasingly facing challenges from civilians who are beginning to hold it responsible for involvement in human rights violations.

Nevertheless, many observers have noted that although Honduras has held regular elections and has begun to hold the military accountable, the nation still faces numerous political challenges, most notably reforming the administration of justice so that both military and civilian elites can be held accountable for their actions, realizing civilian control over the military, and rooting out corruption from government.

The human rights situation deteriorated significantly in the first few years of civilian rule, when the military, under the command of General Gustavo Álvarez Martínez, initiated a campaign against leftists that led to the disappearance of more than 100 people. Small insurgent groups also began operating during this period, but the overwhelming majority of political killings were carried out by the military. Although this violence paled in comparison to the violence in neighboring El Salvador and Guatemala, it marked a departure from the relatively tranquil Honduran political environment. Beginning in 1985, political violence declined significantly but did not completely disappear; a small number of extrajudicial killings continued to be reported annually for the balance of the 1980s and early 1990s. In July 1988 and January 1989, when the Honduran government was held responsible by the Inter-American Court of Human Rights (IACHR) for the 1982 disappearances of Ángel Manfredo Velásquez and Saúl Godínez, Honduran authorities were also held responsible by the court for a deliberate kidnapping campaign of between 100 and 150 individuals believed to be tied to subversive activities between 1981 and 1984.

In the early 1990s, as the political conflicts in El Salvador and Nicaragua were abating, the Honduran public increasingly began to criticize the military for human rights violations, including a number of political and other types of extrajudicial killings. One case that ignited a public outcry against the military was the July 1991 rape, torture, and murder of an eighteen-year old student, Riccy Mabel Martínez, by military members. Initially, the military would not allow the civilian courts to try the three suspects, but ultimately the military discharged the suspects from the military so as not to set the precedent of military members being tried in civilian courts. After a long drawn out process, two of the suspects, including a former colonel, were convicted of the crime in July 1993, marking the first time that a high-ranking officer, even though no longer in the military, was prosecuted in the civilian courts.

Observers credit former United States Ambassador Cresencio Arcos with speaking out promptly on the case and urging the Honduran government to prosecute it through an open judicial process. In fact, the United States embassy increasingly has been viewed as a champion for human rights in Honduras, and its human rights reports in the early 1990s were considerably more critical than those prepared in the 1980s.

Although Honduras has experienced more than a decade of civilian democratic rule, some observers maintain that the military is still the most powerful political player in the country. Its disregard for civilian authority is demonstrated by the military's immunity from prosecution for human rights violations. In early 1993, after the military received considerable public criticism for alleged involvement in the killing of a businessperson in San Pedro Sula in January 1993, military forces were deployed in both San Pedro Sula and in the capital. Rumors abounded about the true intention of the deployment, reportedly made without the knowledge of President Callejas. Some observers speculated that armed forces chief, General Luis Alonso Discua Elvir, took the action to intimidate his opponents and stem a barrage of recent criticism against the military. President Callejas later announced that he had ordered the deployment as one of a series of actions to deter criminal violence.

Some critics maintain that President Callejas should have been more forceful with the military and attempted to assert more civilian control during his presidency, particularly when the military tried to impede the prosecution of the Riccy Martínez case. Some maintain that Callejas himself had close ties with General Discúa, thus explaining why no strong civilian action was taken against the military. Others, however, maintain that Callejas substantially improved civilian control over the military with the establishment of such commissions as the Ad Hoc Commission for Institutional Reform, which recommended the breakup of the National Investigations Department, and the creation of a new Department of Criminal Investigation (Departamento de Investigación Criminal DIC) within the civilian government.

A growing concern of the business sector in the early 1990s was the military's increasing involvement in private enterprise. Through its Military Pension Institute (Instituto de Pensión Militar IPM), the military acquired numerous enterprises, including the nation's largest cement factory, a bank, a real estate agency, cattle ranches, a radio station, and a funeral home. Critics maintain that the military has a competitive advantage in a number of areas because of certain benefits derived from its status, such as the ability to import items duty free.

According to some observers, a fundamental problem associated with the Honduran political system is the almost institutionalized corruption found within its ranks. Analysts maintain that the primary motivation of politicians in Honduras is personal interest; bribery (*la mordida*) is a common or institutionalized practice. Publicized instances of corruption are found throughout the political system, in all branches of government, and some observers maintain that Hondurans have come to expect this of their politicians. As noted by Mark B. Rosenberg, political power in Honduras is defined by one's ability to convert public authority into private advantage. Some analysts contend that corruption is literally a necessity to govern effectively in Honduras. Former United States ambassador Cresencio Arcos notes that "there is more than a kernel of truth in the Latin American cliché, a deal for my friend, the law for my enemies."

Some observers maintain that the Callejas government moderated corrupt practices, as demonstrated by the creation of the Fiscal Intervention Commission that turned its attention to investigating extensive corruption in the Customs Directorate. Others maintain that the commission was a smokescreen to give the appearance that the government was doing something to root out corruption, when in fact the Callejas government was saturated with corruption, and personal enrichment was the norm. The issue of corruption is a theme in the 1993 presidential campaign of PLH candidate Carlos Roberto Reina, who has pledged a moral revolution to punish those public officials enriching themselves through corruption.

Foreign Relations

The conduct of foreign policy in Honduras has traditionally been dominated by the presidency, with the minister of foreign affairs essentially executing that policy. After Honduras returned to civilian rule in 1982, however, the military continued to exercise power over aspects of foreign policy associated with national security. General Gustavo Álvarez reportedly directly negotiated the presence of the anti-Sandinista Contras in Honduras with the United States, as well as the establishment of a United States military presence at Palmerola Air Base and the training of Salvadoran troops at a Regional Center for Military Training in Honduras (Centro Regional de Entrenamiento Militar CREM). Military influence over these aspects of foreign policy continued through the end of the decade, when regional hostilities subsided and reduced Honduras's geostrategic importance for United States policy toward the region.

In the second half of the 1980s, the Ministry of Foreign Affairs, under the dynamic leadership of Carlos López Contreras, reportedly became a professional and well-respected cadre of diplomats. Key positions in the ministry were reportedly chosen on the basis of competence rather than political affiliation. With the change in government in 1990, however, politicization once again became the norm, with preference given to PNH loyalists. President Callejas's active involvement in the regional integration process in Central America has tended to eclipse the prominence of the role of the minister of foreign affairs in the process of formulating foreign policy.

The United States

In the twentieth century, the United States has had more influence on Honduras than any other nation, leading some analysts to assert that the United States has been a major source of political power in Honduras. United States involvement in Honduras dates back to the turn of the century, when United States-owned banana companies began expanding their presence on the north coast. The United States government periodically dispatched warships to quell revolutionary activity and to protect United States business interests. Not long after the United States entered World War II, the United States signed a lend lease agreement with Honduras. Also, the United States operated a small naval base at Trujillo on the Caribbean Sea. In 1954 the two countries signed a bilateral military assistance agreement whereby the United States helped support the development and training of the Honduran military. In the 1950s, the United States provided about US$27 million, largely in development assistance, to Honduras for projects in the agriculture, education, and health sectors. In the 1960s, under the Alliance for Progress program, the United States provided larger amounts of assistance to Honduras almost US$94 million for the decade, the majority again in development assistance, with funds increasingly focused on rural development. In the 1970s, United States assistance expanded significantly, amounting to almost US$193 million, largely in development and food assistance, but also including about US$19 million in military assistance. Aid during the 1970s again emphasized rural development, particularly in support of the

Honduran government's agrarian reform efforts in the first part of the decade.

It was in the 1980s, however, that United States attention became fixated on Honduras as a linchpin for United States policy toward Central America. In the early 1980s, southern Honduras became a staging area for Contra excursions into Nicaragua. The conservative Honduran government and military shared United States concerns over the Sandinistas' military buildup, and both the United States and Honduran governments viewed United States assistance as important in deterring Nicaragua, in both the buildup of the Honduran armed forces and the introduction of a United States military presence in Honduras.

In 1982 Honduras signed an annex to its 1954 bilateral military assistance agreement with the United States that provided for the stationing of a temporary United States military presence in the country. Beginning in 1983, the Pamerola Air Base (renamed the Enrique Soto Cano Air Base in 1988) housed a United States military force of about 1,100 troops known as Joint Task Force Bravo (JTFB) about 80 kilometers from Tegucigalpa near the city of Comayagua. The primary mission of the task force was to support United States military exercises and other military activities and to demonstrate the resolve of the United States to support Honduras against the threat from Nicaragua. In its military exercises, which involved thousands of United States troops and United States National Guardsmen, the United States spent millions of dollars in building or upgrading several air facilities some of which were used to help support the Contras and undertaking roadbuilding projects around the country. The United States military in Honduras also provided medical teams to visit remote rural areas. In addition, a military intelligence battalion performed reconnaissance missions in support of the Salvadoran military in its war against leftist guerrillas of the Farabundo Martí National Liberation Front (Frente Farabundo Martí de Liberación Nacional FMLN). In 1987 the United States approved a sale of twelve advanced F-5 fighter aircraft to Honduras, a measure that reinforced Honduran air superiority in Central America.

During the early 1980s, the United States also established an economic strategy designed to boost economic development in the Caribbean Basin region. Dubbed the Caribbean Basin Initiative (CBI), the centerpiece of the program was a one-way preferential trade program providing duty-free access to the United States market for a large number of products from Caribbean and Central American nations. Honduras became a beneficiary of the program when it first went into effect in 1984. Although the value of Honduran exports had increased by 16 percent by 1989, this growth paled in comparison to the growth of United States-destined exports from other CBI countries such as Costa Rica and the Dominican Republic.

During the 1980s, the United States provided Honduras with a substantial amount of foreign assistance. Total United States assistance to Honduras in the 1980s amounted to almost US$1.6 billion, making the country the largest United States aid recipient in Latin America after El Salvador; about 37 percent of the aid was in Economic Support Funds (ESF), 25 percent in military assistance, 24 percent in development assistance, and 10 percent in food aid. The remaining 4 percent supported one of the largest Peace Corps programs worldwide, disaster assistance, and small development projects sponsored by the Inter-American Foundation.

By the end of the decade, however, critics were questioning how so much money could have produced so little. The country was still one of the poorest in the hemisphere, with an estimated per capita income of US$590 in 1991, according to the World Bank, and the government had not implemented any significant economic reform program to put its house in order. Many high-level Hondurans acknowledged that the money was ill-spent on a military build-up and on easy money for the government. According to former United States ambassador to Honduras Cresencio Arcos, "If there was a significant flaw in our assistance, it was that we did not sufficiently condition aid to macroeconomic reforms and the strengthening of democratic institutions such as the administration of justice." Moreover, as noted by the United States General Accounting Office in a 1989 report, the Honduran government in the 1980s became dependent upon external assistance and tended to view United States assistance as a substitute for undertaking economic reform. The report further asserted that the Honduran government was able to resist implementing economic reforms because it supported United States regional security programs.

Many observers maintain that United States support was instrumental in the early 1980s in bringing about a transition to elected civilian democracy and in holding free and fair elections during the rest of the decade. Nevertheless, critics charge that United States support for the Honduran military, including direct negotiations over support for the Contras, actually worked to undermine the authority of the elected civilian government. They also blame the United States for tolerating the Honduran military's human rights violations, particularly in the early 1980s. They claim that the United States obsession with defeating the Sandinistas in Nicaragua and the FMLN in El Salvador resulted in Honduras's becoming the regional intermediary for United States policy without regard for the consequences for Honduras. Indeed, some maintain that the United States embassy in Tegucigalpa often appeared to be more involved with the Contra war effort against Nicaragua than with the political and economic situation in Honduras. United States-based human rights organizations assert that the United States became involved in a campaign to defame human rights activists in Honduras who called attention to the abuses of the Honduran military. United States embassy publications during the 1980s regularly attempted to discredit the two major human rights groups in Honduras, Codeh and Cofadeh, because of their "leftist bias," while also calling into question the large number of disappearances that occurred in the early 1980s.

Hondurans' frustration over the overwhelming United States presence and power in their country appeared to grow in the late 1980s. For example, in April 1988 a mob of anti-United States rioters attacked and burned the United States embassy annex in Tegucigalpa because of United States involvement in the abduction and arrest of alleged drug trafficker Juan Ramón Mata Ballesteros, a prime suspect in the 1985 torture and murder of United States Drug Enforcement Administration agent Enrique Camarena in Mexico. Nationalist sentiments escalated as some Hondurans viewed the action as a violation of a constitutional prohibition on the extradition of Honduran citizens. The mob of students was reportedly fueled by then UNAH rector Osvaldo Ramos Soto, who later became Supreme Court president and the PNH candidate for president in 1993.

By the early 1990s, with the end to the Contra war and a peace accord in El Salvador, United States policy toward Honduras had changed in numerous respects. Annual foreign aid levels had begun to fall considerably. Although the United States provided about US$213 million in fiscal year (FY) 1990 and US$150 million in FY 1991, the amount declined to about US$98 million for FY 1992 and an estimated US$60 million for FY 1993. Most significant in these declines is that military assistance slowed to a trickle, with only an estimated US$2.6 million to be provided in FY 1993.

Although aid levels were falling, considerable United States support was provided through debt forgiveness. In September 1991, the United States forgave US$434 million in official bilateral debt that Honduras owed the United States government for food assistance and United States AID loans. This forgiveness accounted for about 96 percent of Honduras's total bilateral debt to the United States and about 12 percent of Honduras's total external debt of about US$3.5 billion. Observers viewed the debt forgiveness as partially a reward for Honduras's reliability as a United States ally, particularly through the turbulent 1980s, as well as a sign of support for the bold economic reforms undertaken by the Callejas government in one of the hemisphere's poorest nations.

In the 1990s, the United States remained Honduras's most important trading partner and the most important source of foreign investment. According to the United States Department of State, in the early 1990s Honduras was a relatively open market for United States exports and investments. In 1992 the Callejas government took important steps toward improving the trade and investment climate in the nation with the approval of a new investment law.

Under the rubric of the Enterprise for the Americas Initiative (EAI), a United States foreign policy initiative was introduced by the George H.W. Bush administration (1989-93) in June 1990, with the long-term goal of free trade throughout the Americas. The United States and Honduras signed a trade and investment framework agreement in 1991, which theoretically was a first step on the road to eventual free trade with the United States. Some Hondurans in the early 1990s expressed concern about the potential North American Free Trade Agreement (NAFTA) among Canada, Mexico, and the United States, which could possibly undermine Honduran's benefits under the CBI and also divert portions of United States trade and investment to Mexico.

A point of controversy between Honduras and the United States in the early 1990s was the issue of intellectual property rights. In 1992, because of a complaint by the Motion Picture Exporters Association of America, the Office of the United States Trade Representative (USTR) initiated an investigation into the protection of private satellite television signals. Local cable companies in Honduras routinely pirated United States satellite signals, but as a result of the investigation, the Honduran government pledged to submit comprehensive intellectual property rights legislation to the National Congress in 1993. If the USTR investigation rules against Honduras, the country's participation in the CBI and the Generalized System of Preferences (GSP) would be jeopardized.

A significant change in United States-Honduran relations during the early 1990s was reflected in United States criticism over the human rights situation and over the impunity of the Honduran military, as well as recommendations to the Honduran government to cut back military spending. In one public statement in 1992 that was severely criticized by the Honduran military, Cresencio Arcos, who was then United States ambassador, stated that "society should not allow justice to be turned into a viper that only bites the barefoot and leaves immune those who wear boots."

Despite the winding down of regional conflicts in the early 1990s, the United States military maintains a 1,100-member force presence at the Enrique Soto Cano Air Base. Joint Task Force Bravo is still involved in conducting training exercises for thousands of United States troops annually, including road-building exercises, and in providing medical assistance to remote rural areas. A new mission for the United States military in Honduras, and perhaps its number-one priority, is the use of surveillance planes to track drug flights from South America headed for the United States. Although Honduras is not a major drug producer, it is a transit route for cocaine destined for both the United States and Europe. A radar station in Trujillo on the north Honduran coast forms part of a Caribbean-wide radar network designed for the interdiction of drug traffickers. The United States military in Honduras maintains a relatively low profile, with soldiers confined to the base, and the sporadic anti-Americanism targeted at the United States military in the past appears largely to have dissipated, most probably because of the end to regional hostilities and the new supportive role of the United States as an advocate for the protection of human rights.

Central America

Honduran national hero Francisco Morazán was a prominent leader of the United Provinces Central America in the 1820s and 1830s, but his vision of a united Central America was never fully realized because of divisiveness among the five original member nations Costa Rica, El Salvador, Guatemala, Honduras, and Nicaragua each of which went its separate way in 1838 with the official breakup of the federation. Subsequent hopes of restoring some type of political union were unsuccessful until the 1960s, when economic integration efforts led to the formation of the Central American Common Market (CACM). In December 1960, the General Treaty of Central American Integration was signed by El Salvador, Guatemala, Honduras, and Nicaragua, and the CACM became effective in June 1961. One year later, Costa Rica acceded to the treaty.

The objectives of the CACM are to eliminate trade barriers among the five countries and institute a common external tariff (CET). Two important institutions were established as a result of CACM economic integration efforts in the 1960s. One was the Secretariat of the General Treaty on Central American Economic Integration (Secretaría Permanente del Tratado General de Integración Económica Centroamericana SIECA), based in Guatemala City, which serves as the CACM's executive organ. The other was the Central American Bank for Economic Integration (Banco Centroamericano de Integración Económica BCIE) headquartered in Tegucigalpa, which is the CACM's financial institution that lends funds to its member nations, particularly for infrastructure projects. The CACM integration process was somewhat successful in the 1960s, but by the end of the decade essentially fell into disarray because of the 1969 border war between Honduras and El Salvador, the so-called "Soccer War". Honduras officially suspended its participation in the CACM in December 1970, and relations with El Salvador remained tense in the 1970s, with border hostilities flaring up in 1976.

A peace treaty between Honduras and El Salvador was finally signed in 1980, reportedly under significant pressure from the United States. According to political scientist Ernesto Paz Aguilar, the treaty allied the Honduran and Salvadoran government in a campaign against the leftist Salvadoran insurgents, as evidenced by the Honduran military's participation in the Río Sumpul massacre of Salvadoran peasants in April 1980, when hundreds of Salvadoran peasants were reportedly killed as they attempted to cross the river into Honduras.

Given the historical animosity between the two nations, this military alliance was indeed surprising. As noted by Victor Meza, United States policy demanded "ideological and operational solidarity with a country [El Salvador]" with which there existed "a territorial dispute and an historic antagonism." For Honduras, United States military assistance would benefit Honduras not only in case of conflict with Nicaragua, but also, perhaps most importantly, in case of conflict with El Salvador. One example of United States disregard for Honduran sensitivities was the establishment of a Regional Center for Military Training at Puerto Castilla in 1983, primarily to train Salvadoran soldiers. The center was eventually closed in 1985 after General Álvarez Martínez, who had agreed to the establishment of the center, was ousted by General López Reyes. The official Salvadoran-Honduran bilateral relationship gradually improved in the 1980s.

In the early 1990s, there was considerable movement toward integration in Central America, in part because of the good personal relations among the Central American presidents. The semiannual Central American presidential summits became institutionalized and were complemented by numerous other meetings among two or more of the region's nations. The so-called northern triangle of Central America, consisting of Guatemala, El Salvador, and Honduras, made consistently stronger efforts toward integration than did Costa Rica or Nicaragua. At the tenth Central American summit held in San Salvador in July 1991, the presidents decided to incorporate Panama into the integration process, although the method by which this would occur had not been spelled out as of mid-1993. Belize has also attended the semiannual summits as an observer. Although Honduras actively participated in Central American summits since 1986, it officially rejoined the integration process in February 1992, when the Transitional Multilateral Free

Trade Agreement between Honduras and the other Central American states came into force.

The rejuvenation of economic integration began in June 1990 at the eighth presidential summit held in Antigua, Guatemala, when the presidents pledged to restructure, strengthen, and reactivate the integration process. The presidents signed a Central American Economic Action Plan (Plan de Acción Económica de Centroamérica Paeca) that included a number of commitments and guidelines for integration. These included such varied measures as elimination of intraregional tariff barriers; support for commercial integration; tightening of regional coordination for external trade, foreign investment, and tourism; promotion of industrial restructuring; formulation and application of coordinated agricultural and science and technology policies; and promotion of coordinated macroeconomic adjustment processes.

At the eleventh presidential summit held in December 1991 in Tegucigalpa, the presidents signed a protocol for the establishment of the Central American Integration System (Sistema de Integración Centroamericana Sica) to serve as a governing body for the integration process. The protocol was ratified by the Central American states, and Sica began operating in February 1993. The main objective of Sica is to coordinate the region's integration institutions, including SIECA and the BCIE, which were established in the 1960s.

Further progress toward economic integration was achieved in January 1993, when the five Central American states agreed to reduce the maximum external tariff for third countries from 40 to 20 percent. In April 1993, a new Central American Free Trade Zone went into effect among the three northern triangle states and Nicaragua. The new grouping reduced tariffs for intraregional trade to the 5-20 percent range for some 5,000 products, with the intention of lowering the tariff levels and expanding the scope of product coverage. The northern triangle states agreed to create a free trade area and customs union by April 1994.

As regards political integration, the Central American presidents in 1987 signed a Constituent Treaty to set up a Central American Parliament (Parlamento Centroamericano Parlacen) to serve as a deliberative body that would support integration and democracy through consultations and recommendations. With the exception of Costa Rica, the other four Central American countries approved the treaty, and Parlacen was approved in September 1988. Each country was to have twenty elected deputies in the parliament, but by the date of its inauguration in October 1991, only three nations Honduras, El Salvador, and Guatemala had elected representatives. Nicaragua planned to elect deputies by early 1994. Costa Rica's participation in Parlacen was impeded by domestic opposition. Since February 1993, Parlacen has formed part of Sica. Other political organizations under Sica are the Central American Court of Justice and the Consultative Committee, consisting of representatives from different social sectors.

As illustrated by the integration process, Honduras's relations with El Salvador and Nicaragua were close in the early 1990s. In September 1992, after six years of consideration, the ICJ ruled on the border dispute with El Salvador and awarded Honduras approximately two-thirds of the disputed area. Both countries agreed to abide by the decision. The ruling was viewed as a victory for Honduras, but also one that provided Honduras with significant challenges in dealing with the nearly 15,000 residents of the disputed *bolsones* who identified themselves as Salvadorans. Residents of the *bolsones* petitioned both governments in 1992 for land rights, freedom of movement between both nations, and the preservation of community organizations. A Honduran-Salvadoran Binational Commission was set up to work out any disputes. The ICJ also determined that El Salvador, Honduras, and Nicaragua were to share control of the Golfo de Fonseca on the Pacific coast. El Salvador was awarded the islands of Meanguera and Meanguerita, and Honduras was awarded the island of El Tigre.

In 1993 political conflict in Nicaragua was again on the rise, with the government of President Chamorro struggling to achieve national reconciliation between conservatives of her former ruling coalition and the leftist Sandinistas. Conservative critics of Chamorro charged her with caving in to Sandinista demands and complained that the Sandinistas still controlled the military and policy. Rearmed former Contras were forming in northern Nicaragua, with reported support from Nicaraguan and Cuban communities in the United States. Memories of the early 1980s led some observers to fear a flare-up of hostilities in the Honduran-Nicaraguan border area, as well as the prospect of another flood of Nicaraguan refugees into Honduras. Political observers and most Hondurans were hopeful, however, that even should turmoil break out in neighboring countries, Honduras would be able to follow the course laid out in the 1980s and continue to strengthen its democratic   traditions.

Made in United States
Orlando, FL
19 May 2022

18012194R00124